Cookbook

The
CHEFS
EDITION
••••••

With
BRICKWOOD
GALUTERIA
••••••

Photography
BRETT
UPRICHARD
••••••

WATERMARK
PUBLISHING

Hawai'i's Kitchen trade name and service mark © KHON2

ISBN 0-9742672-2-8

Library of Congress Control Number: 2003114120

Design
Leo Gonzalez

Production
Wendy Wakabayashi

Watermark Publishing
1088 Bishop Street, Suite 310
Honolulu, HI 96813
Telephone: Toll-free 1-866-900-BOOK
Web site: www.bookshawaii.net
e-mail: sales@bookshawaii.net

Printed in the Republic of Korea

Contents

Acknowledgments

First, I want to thank our guest chefs: Chai Chaowasaree, Glenn Chu, Hiroshi Fukui, Beverly Gannon, D.K. Kodama, George Mavrothalassitis, Colin Nishida, Russell Siu, Alan Wong and Linda Yamada. I'm honored that these busy folks would lend their time and talents to make this book possible. It wasn't easy selecting ten chefs from Hawai'i's galaxy of star chefs. In fact, it was nearly impossible. (But hey, that's a great reason to do a sequel, right? Attention *Hawai'i's Kitchen* chefs who aren't in this edition: Expect a call from us any day now!)

I also want to acknowledge and thank Jan Nagano, my project coordinator. Her organizational skills and enthusiasm made her perfect for this project.

Another big mahalo to KHON2 General Manager Rick Blangiardi, the KHON2 ohana and the entire crew of *Hawai'i's Kitchen*. Plain and simple, they are a joy to work with.

Thanks also to George Engebretson, Donovan Dela Cruz and Leo Gonzalez — my newfound partners at Watermark Publishing; Brett Uprichard, who took all the beautiful photos you see in this book; and Rodney Lau of Hawai'i Wholesale Travelers.

Last but certainly not least, I want to extend my warmest mahalo to all of you who have watched and supported *Hawai'i's Kitchen* these past five years. We're here today because of you.

Mahalo and Aloha!

Inside *Hawai'i's Kitchen*

I n late 1997 the folks at KHON2 called me with an idea.

"Let's meet as soon as possible," they said. "We want to talk to you about hosting a show for us."

Okay, I thought, this might be something good.

On the way to the television station, I let my imagination run. What kind of show were they thinking of? A talk show, maybe? A musical variety show? Maybe some type of community-based program?

Little did I realize that what they envisioned combined elements from all of the above — blended together in the form of a cooking show!

That turned out to be one interesting meeting. KHON2 was excited about the possibilities, but I wasn't quite as sold. I could see that the show itself had a lot of potential, but a cooking show with Brickwood Galuteria as host? I'll be honest with you: In those days, I had a hard time boiling water!

Nevertheless, I signed on, and *Hawai'i's Kitchen* was born. I remember the first show with great fondness. It debuted on March 8, 1998, and our very first guest was then-First Lady Vicky Cayetano. We wanted our debut to be a special one, we reasoned, so why not tape it at

Washington Place, inside Hawai'i's "First Kitchen"?

Vicky was gracious enough to welcome the crew in, and it was a fantastic way to unveil our program. She wanted to give us a healthy menu, so her recipes included Sugar Snap Peas, Tofu Stir Fry and Fresh Apple Spice Cake. Meanwhile, I was having a ball in my admittedly unique surroundings. "Here I am in the First Kitchen," I announced. "I am holding the First Spatula. I am now opening the First Oven..."

Man, how time flies. Has it really been five years?

No doubt about it, *Hawai'i's Kitchen* has come a long way. We've done more than 200 shows, and we're still going strong. If you're a faithful viewer of our program (and if you're not, we love you anyway), you've gotten to "taste" all the flavors served up by people in our Island community. You've seen Frank De Lima make De Lima's Bachelor Stew and Fried Saimin Ala De Lima. You've seen Na Leo Pilimehana put together a Salmon Tofu Salad and 'Ahi Teri Miso. You've even seen professional wrestlers Sick Dog, J.T. Wolfen and the "Hawaiian Gods of Destruction" (Tiki and Bruiser) concoct Garlic Clam Pasta Diablo and something called H-Gods' Honey Garlic Ribs.

From firefighters and bank executives to recording artists and radio personalities, *Hawai'i's Kitchen* has embraced folks from all walks of life. Really, I think that's been one of the secrets to the show's success. We're not afraid to go off in many different directions.

Me? I'm just grateful to be a part of this whole thing. This is *Hawai'i's Kitchen*, after all, not *Brickwood's Kitchen*. I just happen to hang out in everybody's kitchen every week.

From the very start, however, I knew I needed something to serve as my "signature" for the show. It certainly wasn't going to be my cooking! (Five years later, thankfully, I can now cook a dish or two.) Then I remembered Graham Kerr on "The Galloping Gourmet." I used to wait for him to sample the food because he'd really savor every bite. It made me want to be there, and I lived vicariously through him. So I decided that would be my role on *Hawai'i's Kitchen*, too. I would taste the food. (Hey, as the saying goes, it's a tough job, but...)

I think *Hawai'i's Kitchen* is a great and unique show. It's something that the people of Hawai'i can be proud of. It reminds us, "Yes, we can wear tuxedos and zori slippers at the same time." I like to call the food on our show Kanaka Nouvelle Cuisine!

Obviously, we must be doing something right. We have a faithful following of viewers every week. We have a long list of people wanting to appear on our program. And now we have our first-ever cookbook with nearly 100 recipes, many of them from past shows. We hope you enjoy them. This book, I think, is an appropriate way to celebrate and reflect on our first five years of *Hawai'i's Kitchen*.

Aloha no!

Chai Chaowasaree

CHAI'S
ALOHA TOWER MARKETPLACE
ISLAND BISTRO

Chai is one of those chefs who make everything look effortless. He's like a magician, and some of his dishes are real sleight-of-hand stuff. He puts so much into his cooking, yet he makes it look easy.

One time, for example, Chai prepared his Pork Osso Bucco on our show. The recipe called for everything but the kitchen sink! It had shallots, shiitake mushrooms, coriander roots, star anise, sticks of cinnamon, licorice root, bay leaves, paprika — you name it. He put together this great dish, but I thought to myself, "I know it just happened in front of me, but how did he do that?"

If you've been to the Aloha Tower Marketplace, you probably know about Chai's Island Bistro, which serves contemporary Island and Pacific Rim cuisine. The restaurant has received glowing reviews from major magazines like *Bon Appétit, Sunset, Travel & Leisure* and *Gourmet*. Chai also owns, along with his sisters, Singha Thai Cuisine in Waikīkī, another award-winning restaurant.

Chai himself has cooked for the prime ministers of Thailand and Indonesia, the Princess of Thailand, the King and Queen of Malaysia, and many other luminaries.

I love having Chai on *Hawai'i's Kitchen*. He's a nice, personable guy, and he's got plenty of aloha. He's also a very meticulous chef, for whom everything has to be just right. He's the kind of guy who likes to welcome everybody in. He's very outgoing and has a good sense of humor.

Of course, to go through what Chai went through, you've got to have a sense of humor. If you remember, the chef ran into some immigration troubles a few years ago, and he had to fight to stay in the U.S. He even had to spend some time in jail.

When I see Chai these days, I like to joke with him: I tell him that he should've cooked for the warden! At least a couple of dishes, y'know? Once I asked him, "How was the food in there?" and he told me, "The food was real good."

Maybe it was. But I doubt it was "Chai level."

Fresh Kona Lobster with Chili-Ginger Sauce

1 lb.	kabocha pumpkin
1-1/2 lbs.	fresh Kona lobster
	flour for dusting
1 cup	vegetable oil

Chili-Ginger Sauce

1 clove	garlic, chopped
1/2 tbsp.	chili paste in oil (prik prao), to taste
1 tbsp.	vegetable oil
1/4 cup	hot water or chicken stock
1 tbsp.	oyster sauce
1 tbsp.	diced bell pepper
1 tbsp.	diced red onion
1 tbsp.	sliced green onion
dash	sugar

Peel and clean pumpkin, removing all seeds. Cut into bite-sized pieces, 1 to 2 inches. Steam over high heat for 5 to 10 minutes, depending on thickness, until the pumpkin is easily pierced with a bamboo stick or small knife. Mash the pumpkin; set aside. Clean the lobster and cut in half from head to tail. Leave the shell on and coat with flour. Heat the oil in a wok or deep fryer to 375 degrees. Deep-fry the lobster until it turns light brown, about 1-1/2 minutes. Set aside. To prepare the sauce: Saute the garlic and chili paste with in vegetable oil for about 1 minute (be sure the garlic does not burn). Add hot water and oyster sauce. Boil for 1 to 2 minutes. Add the lobster, bell pepper, red and green onions, and sugar to the sauce. Cook for 1 more minute, until the sauce is absorbed into the lobster and vegetables. To serve: Place the mashed pumpkin in the center of a plate, then top with lobster, with sauce spooned around the sides. Serves 1. Note: Scallops, shrimp or fresh fish may be substituted for the lobster.

Kataifi and Macadamia Nut-Crusted Kaua'i Prawns with Big Island Baby Greens and Pineapple Vinaigrette

8	Kauai shrimp (or jumbo black tiger prawns), peeled
1/4 tbsp.	lemon juice
	salt and pepper, to taste
8	bamboo sticks
2 tbsp.	flour
1 tbsp.	cornstarch
1 tbsp.	chopped macadamia nuts
1	egg
4 tbsp.	cold water
1 box	kataifi (shredded filo dough) or any thin noodles
4 cups	vegetable oil
	baby greens, for garnish
	pineapple spear, for garnish

Pineapple Vinaigrette
1/2 cup	pineapple juice
1 tbsp.	sugar
1 tbsp.	white vinegar
	salt, to taste
dash	Tabasco sauce

To prepare the vinaigrette: Combine all the ingredients in a pot. Bring to a boil, then reduce heat and simmer for a few minutes. Cool to room temperature. Toss the shrimp with the lemon juice, salt and pepper (the acid from the lemon juice makes the shrimp crunchy). Skewer the shrimp on the bamboo sticks; set aside. Combine the flour, cornstarch, macadamia nuts, egg and cold water. Dip the prawns in the batter, then wrap with the kataifi. Heat the oil in a wok or deep fryer to 375 degrees. Fry the prawns for a few minutes, until light brown. Pour vinaigrette over prawns just before serving; garnish with baby greens and pineapple spear. Serves 4.

Fresh Salmon Tartare with Lemon-Dill Cream Sauce

1-3/4 tbsp. chopped fresh dill
6 tbsp.   sugar
3 tbsp.   salt
1 tbsp.   grated lemon zest
1   salmon fillet (about 3 lbs.)
            lemon slice, sliced cucumber, black and red
                caviar, for garnish

Lemon-Dill Cream Sauce
4 tbsp.   sour cream
1 tbsp.   dijon mustard
2 tbsp.   lemon juice
1/4 tbsp.   chopped fresh dill
            salt and pepper, to taste

Combine the dill with the sugar, salt and lemon zest.
Coat the salmon evenly on both sides with the seasoning
mix. Allow the salmon to cure overnight, or at least 4 hours.
Thoroughly remove seasoning from the salmon, then chop
salmon into little pieces. Set aside. To prepare the dill sauce:
Combine the sour cream, mustard, lemon juice, dill, salt and
pepper. Mix 3/4 of the sauce with the chopped salmon.
Garnish with a lemon slice, cucumber, caviar and more dill.
Serve with toast pieces or crackers, with the remaining
sauce on the side. Serves 10.

Blackened 'Ahi Summer Rolls with Soy-Ginger Sesame Sauce

4 strips	fresh 'ahi, about 10 inches long (3 oz. each)
	Cajun spice, to taste
4 pieces	Thai rice paper (12-inch size)
	enoki mushrooms, for garnish
	radish sprouts, for garnish
1 oz.	shredded carrots
1 oz.	shredded beets
1 oz.	shredded green mango
16	mint leaves
4 oz.	baby lettuce

Sprinkle the fish strips with Cajun spice. In a hot nonstick pan, sear the fish for about 30 seconds. Set aside. Soften each piece of rice paper by spraying it with water or covering it with a damp cloth for about 30 seconds. Lay the rice paper on a flat surface. At one end of each sheet layer the enoki mushrooms and radish sprouts, followed by the carrots, beets, green mango, mint leaves, 1 piece of 'ahi and some baby lettuce. Roll rice paper into a tube with ingredients inside. Cut roll into bite-sized pieces.

Soy-Ginger Sesame Sauce

1 cup	low sodium soy sauce (less if preferred)
1 cup	cooking mirin (Japanese sweet rice wine)
1 cup	water
1 oz.	sliced fresh ginger
1 oz.	sliced onions
1 oz.	sliced celery
1 oz.	sliced carrot
dash	sesame oil
2 tbsp.	unsalted butter, at room temperature

Place all the ingredients except butter into a pot. Bring to a boil, then reduce heat and simmer for 20 to 30 minutes. Strain, then return the strained sauce to the pot. Slowly add the butter to the sauce, whipping continuously until incorporated. Immediately remove from heat.

Tom Yum Spicy Lemongrass Soup with Shrimp

3 cups	chicken stock
2 stalks	lemongrass, sliced
8	kaffir lime leaves
1 clove	shallot
1 clove	garlic
2	cherry tomato, halved
10	large shrimp, peeled and cleaned
1/2 cup	straw or button mushrooms
1/4 tbsp.	sugar
1/2 tbsp.	fish sauce
1/2 tbsp.	chili paste in oil (prik pao)
1 tbsp.	lime or lemon juice
	fresh chili pepper, optional
1 tbsp.	cilantro

Combine chicken stock, lemongrass, lime leaves, shallot, garlic and cherry tomato in a pot; bring to a boil. Add shrimp, mushrooms, sugar, fish sauce and chili paste. Continue to boil just until the shrimp is done (do not overcook). Just before serving add the lime juice, fresh chili and cilantro. Serves 2. Note: Any meat, seafood or vegetable may be substituted for the shrimp.

Siamese Fighting Fish with Spicy Chili Sauce

1 to 2 lb.	snapper or any whole fresh fish, cleaned
	flour, for dusting
4 cups	vegetable oil

Spicy Chili Sauce

1 clove	garlic, chopped
1 oz.	sliced red onion
1 clove	shallot, sliced
2 tbsp.	vegetable oil
1 oz.	sliced carrot
1 oz.	sliced bell pepper
2 oz.	sliced celery
	chili pepper, to taste
3 tbsp.	fish sauce or low-sodium soy sauce
2 tbsp.	sugar
2 tbsp.	lime juice

Heat the oil in a wok or deep fryer to 375 degrees. Coat the fish in flour and deep-fry until golden brown. To prepare the sauce: Saute the garlic, onion and shallot in vegetable oil for 30 seconds, until onions are translucent. Add the vegetables and chili pepper; saute for about 2 minutes. Add the fish sauce and sugar; saute for 30 seconds. Add the lime juice and turn off the heat (overcooking the acid in the lime can turn the sauce bitter). Pour the Spicy Chili Sauce on top of the crispy fried fish. Serves 1 to 2.

Maui Onion Demiglace for Steak

1 cup	Maui onions, sliced
1 cup	shiitake mushrooms, sliced
1 tbsp.	vegetable oil
1 cup	red wine
1 cup	veal stock
2 tbsp.	unsalted butter
	salt and pepper, to taste

On medium heat, saute Maui onions in vegetable oil to caramelize the onions, about 2-4 minutes, then add red wine. Let boil to reduce the wine until wine almost disappears. Add veal stock. Bring to a boil on high heat, then add mushrooms. Cook for a minute or so. Add butter, salt and pepper. Serve on top of any steak.

Glenn Chu

INDIGO

I think of Glenn Chu as Hawai'i's premier martial artist of cuisine. Maybe it's because he seems to approach his work as a martial arts form, where every dish has a special meaning in life. (Right now, I'm visualizing Glenn standing in the White Crane position!)

I don't think there's any hidden secret behind the success of his award-winning restaurant, Indigo Eurasian Cuisine. The food is just amazing! When people talk about the revitalization of Chinatown in downtown Honolulu, they

usually point to the reopening of the Hawaii Theatre — and rightfully so. But Indigo was around even before the theater reopened, and I think Glenn should get some credit, too, because Indigo has also become a leader on the downtown social scene.

From what I understand, Glenn's earliest "food memories" are of his grandmother who grew her own vegetables in her Mānoa garden and cooked big-time meals for the family in her giant wok. Large family functions often required two full days of cooking, and young Glenn would watch, learn and sometimes lend a helping hand. Glenn was also influenced by Julia Child's cooking shows in the 1960s. As an eight-year-old, in fact, Glenn was inspired to try his hand at making cream puffs just the way Julia Child made them. He did an excellent job, he recalls, except for one minor slip: He forgot the filling.

Like many successful chefs, Glenn ventured out into the world to expand and sharpen his culinary talents. Greek and Italian cooking were major influences when he lived in Detroit. Subsequent travels took him throughout the U.S., Europe and Asia. He calls Indigo the fulfillment of his dream to open his own Chinese restaurant.

But Indigo isn't your ordinary Chinese eatery. Its menu combines all of Glenn's experience in Eastern and Western cuisines. Glenn says the resulting cuisine is more than the sum of its parts. If you've ever eaten there,  you know what he means. It's good stuff.

As a chef, Glenn is very demanding — perfectionists always are — yet he's also extremely caring. And as a guest on my show, he's someone who'll dance along with you. He likes to joke and fool around. That's what makes Glenn one of my favorite chefs to host on *Hawai'i's Kitchen*.

Coconut Haupia Meringue Torte

Meringue
7	egg whites, at room temperature
2-1/2 cups	powdered sugar, sifted
1 tsp.	cream of tartar
1/2 cup	sweetened coconut flakes

Haupia Mousse
1/2 cup	unsweetened coconut milk
1 package	unflavored gelatin
4	egg yolks
1/2 cup	sugar
2 cups	heavy whipping cream
1/2 cup	sweetened coconut flakes
	powdered sugar (optional)

Preheat oven to 325 degrees. For meringue: In an electric mixer on high speed, whip the egg whites for 2 minutes or until they become fluffy, white and semi-stiff. Decrease the mixer speed to low; add the powdered sugar and cream of tartar and mix until all the sugar is incorporated. Increase the mixer speed to high again, and beat for another 8 minutes, until the egg whites are very stiff. Gently fold in the coconut. Transfer the mixture into a pastry bag fitted with a 1-inch plain tip. On a parchment paper-lined baking sheet, draw 3 8-inch coiled circles, starting at the middle of each circle. On another parchment paper-lined baking sheet, draw 4 to 6 parallel lines of meringue. Bake the meringue in the middle of the oven for 45 minutes or until it is very dry. Cool, then remove from the parchment. (The meringue can be stored in a cool, dry place for up to 1 week. If it becomes soft, bake for 10 minutes at 325 degrees until dry and crisp.) For the mousse: In a small bowl, combine 1/4 cup coconut milk and gelatin for 5 minutes until the gelatin has dissolved. In a small saucepan on medium heat, gently heat the remaining 1/4 cup coconut milk until simmering; remove from heat. Blend the gelatin mixture into the hot milk. Using an electric mixer fitted with a whip, beat the egg yolks and 1/4 cup of sugar on high speed for 5 minutes until the yolks are yellow and fluffy; set aside. Using a clean bowl and whip, whip the cream for 2 minutes on high; reduce the speed to low, and add the remaining 1/4 cup of sugar. Continue beating for another minute until fluffy and stiff. In a medium bowl, combine the egg yolk and coconut milk mixtures. Gently fold in the cream and the coconut flakes. Cover with plastic wrap and refrigerate for 10 minutes until cool. To assemble: Position a meringue circle onto a dinner-sized plate or platter. With a pastry bag fitted with a 1-inch plain tip, squeeze a 1-inch layer of mousse evenly over the circle. Place another meringue circle on top of the mousse, and repeat with another layer of mousse. Top with the final meringue layer, and cover the entire cake, including top and sides, with a 1-inch layer of mousse. Refrigerate until ready to serve. (The cake can also be frozen for up to a week at this point.) Just before serving, break the straight pieces of meringue into 2-inch long segments; cover the top and sides of the cake with the pieces, allowing the ends to stick out of the cake, creating a porcupine effect. Dust with powdered sugar. Serve immediately. Serves 10 to 12.

Black Peppercorn Spiced Veal Cheeks

2 lbs.	veal cheeks
1 8-inch piece	fresh ginger (about10 ounces), smashed
2-1/2 cups	brown sugar, packed
3 tbsp.	whole black peppercorns
3 pieces	star anise
20	dried chili peppers
8	bay leaves
16 cloves	garlic
1/2 cup	low-sodium sauce, preferably Aloha brand
1/2 cup	apple cider vinegar
4 cups	water

Place all the ingredients in a Dutch oven, casserole or large baking pan. Bring to a boil; reduce heat to a low simmer and partially cover. Cook for 2 hours, skimming frequently, or until the meat becomes very soft. Remove from heat and discard the ginger. Transfer the veal cheeks to another dish and set aside. Skim the oil from the braising liquid. Return the liquid to a boil; decrease heat to a simmer and cook for 15 minutes or until the liquid is reduced by 10 percent. Remove from heat. Return the veal cheeks to the sauce until they are hot again. Serve immediately with rice and a little pickled ginger. Serves 4.

Steamed Moloka'i Peaberry Coffee Creme Brulee

4 tbsp.	ground Moloka'i Peaberry Coffee or other full-bodied ground coffee
2-1/2 cups	half and half
1/4 cup	palm sugar
2	cinnamon sticks
1/8 tsp.	freshly ground nutmeg
5	egg yolks, lightly beaten
8 tsp.	sugar

Place the coffee, half and half, palm sugar, cinnamon sticks and nutmeg into a saucepan. Bring to a boil; reduce heat to low and simmer 10 minutes. Remove from heat, and strain through a fine-mesh strainer. Allow the mixture to cool slightly, then slowly add egg yolks, stirring constantly. Divide the mixture evenly among 4 ramekins or coffee cups (4-1/2 oz. size). Prepare a steamer. Place the ramekins in the bottom of the steamer; cover and steam for 20 minutes, until firm. Remove ramekins from the steamer and let cool. Cover and refrigerate until ready to serve. To serve, sprinkle 2 tsp. of sugar evenly over the top of each creme brulee. Using a hand-held kitchen blowtorch, caramelize the sugar until browned and bubbling, 20 to 30 seconds. Or, place the ramekins in a roasting pan filled with ice. Place under a hot broiler until the sugar is browned and bubbling, 1 to 2 minutes, watching carefully so sugar does not burn. Serve immediately. Serves 4.

Ten Thousand Chili Fried Moi

4	skinless, boneless moi fillets (6 to 8 oz. each) or other mild white-fleshed fish
	kosher salt, to taste
	freshly ground black pepper, to taste
3 cups	olive oil
2 cups	dried red chilies

Breading

1 cup	panko
2 tbsp.	Szechuan peppercorns (optional)
1/2 tsp.	kosher salt
1/2 cup	flour
1/2 tsp.	freshly ground black pepper
2	eggs, beaten

Yogurt Mustard Seed Sauce

1/2 tsp.	cumin seeds
1/2 tsp.	black or brown mustard seeds
1 cup	plain yogurt
1 tbsp.	chopped cilantro
1 tbsp.	chopped mint
1 tsp.	fresh lemon juice
1/2 tsp.	kosher salt
1/2 tsp.	finely diced jalapeno pepper

For yogurt sauce: In a small saute pan, toast the cumin and mustard seeds over high heat until mustard seeds become fragrant and begin to pop. Combine the toasted spices with the remaining ingredients. Cover and refrigerate until ready to use. For the fish: Season both sides of the fish with salt and pepper. Cut the fillets diagonally into 3/4-inch slices. For breading: Combine the panko, Szechuan peppercorns and salt in a shallow bowl. Place the flour and black pepper in a second shallow bowl and the beaten egg in a third shallow bowl. Dredge the fillets in flour, shaking off any excess, then dip in egg, shaking off excess, and dredge in the panko mixture. Heat the oil to 325 degrees in a wok, a heavy, flameproof casserole or deep-fryer. Add chilies and cook until chilies turn dark, 3 to 5 minutes. Using a wire mesh skimmer, transfer the chilies to a plate lined with paper towels; set aside. Increase the oil temperature to 365 degrees. Fry fish in the chili-infused oil without crowding, turning occasionally, until crisp and golden, about 3 minutes. Using a wire mesh skimmer, transfer the fish to a plate lined with paper towels; drain. Serve immediately with Yogurt Mustard Seed Sauce and garnish with a few reserved red chilies. Serves 4.

Popo's Tofu

3 tbsp.	olive oil
2 tsp.	minced garlic
15	dried red chilies
1/2 tsp.	Szechuan peppercorns (optional)
1/8 tsp.	saffron threads (optional)
2 tbsp.	thin soy sauce
1 lb.	soft tofu, drained, cut into 1-inch cubes
1/4 tsp.	kosher salt
1/4 tsp.	freshly ground black pepper
2 tbsp.	sliced green onion, green part only
1 tsp.	sesame oil

In a large saute pan, heat the olive oil over high heat.
Add the garlic and cook, stirring constantly, until lightly
browned, about 1 minute. Add the dried chilies, Szechuan
peppercorns and saffron; cook 1 minute to infuse the oil.
Add the soy sauce and cook until slightly reduced, about
1 minute. Add tofu, salt and pepper; cook 2 minutes.
Gently turn the tofu and cook an additional 2 minutes.
Add green onions and sesame oil; and heat through.
Serve family-style, in a shallow bowl, accompanied by rice.
Serves 4.

Green Papaya Salad with Shrimp Splashed with Tangerine Sauce

1	medium green papaya, peeled, halved and seeded
1/2 tsp.	kosher salt
	freshly ground black pepper, to taste
1 tbsp.	Heaven and Earth brand Tangerine Sauce or orange juice concentrate
1/2 tsp.	sesame oil
1 tbsp.	sherry vinegar
1 tbsp.	chopped cilantro
1 tbsp.	chopped chives
1/2 tsp.	black sesame seeds
2	ripe papayas, halved and seeded
16	jumbo shrimp, cooked, peeled and deveined

Grate the green papaya into fine julienne, and place into a medium-sized bowl. Season with salt and pepper. Add the Tangerine Sauce, sesame oil and sherry vinegar. Sprinkle with the cilantro, chives and black sesame seeds; toss gently. (The salad may be covered and stored up to 2 hours in the refrigerator at this point). Just before serving, divide the green papaya salad evenly among the ripe papaya halves, and top each with 4 shrimp. Serve immediately. Serves 4.

Dragon Fire Salmon

3 tbsp.	brown sugar
1 tbsp.	fresh lime juice
6 tbsp.	Heaven and Earth brand Dragon Fire Sauce or other hot sauce
4	salmon fillets, 5 ounces each
	kosher salt and freshly ground black pepper, to taste
2 tbsp.	olive oil
1 cup	thinly sliced red bell pepper
1 cup	thinly sliced green bell pepper
1 cup	thinly sliced red onion
1	medium tomato, sliced into 4 slices
3 tbsp.	chopped cilantro

Blend together the sugar, lime juice and hot sauce; set aside. Season the salmon with salt and pepper. Heat a medium-sized saute pan or wok over high heat until very hot. Add the oil. Sear the fillets, skin side down, for about 1 minute, until lightly browned. Gently turn the salmon. Add the green and red peppers, red onions, tomato and the sauce to the pan; cover, reduce the heat to low, and cook about 3 minutes, or until the fish is cooked through. Remove the fish and set aside. Garnish with chopped cilantro. Serve immediately with the vegetables and steamed rice. Serves 4.

Hiroshi Fukui

C hef Hiroshi can be a hard man to grab hold of these days. You see, it's hard to catch a rising star.

It's always interesting to see different chefs at different stages of their careers. Hiroshi is one of Hawai'i's young, up-and-coming chefs. Born in Japan and raised in the Islands, he was trained in the *kaiseki* tradition (formal cooking style) of Japanese cuisine. Anyone who's savored lunch or dinner at L'Uraku — and I have many times — will recognize Hiroshi's superb talent for combining fresh Island ingredi-

ents, traditional Japanese training and distinctive European influences. As HONOLULU Magazine editor John Heckathorn put it, "Hiroshi Fukui may not be a household name — yet — but he can cook with the best."

Hiroshi takes his work seriously. My first impression of him, in fact, was how humble he was—almost Buddha-like! Even today, I compare Hiroshi to a guy who's into the Zen of cooking; I can see him walking on a path of culinary enlightenment!

Through it all, however, this Kaimukī High School alum has kept a very humble attitude. It's almost as though he's awed by his own success. He may be a star on the rise, but I'm not sure he believes his own promo.

That kind of humility sometimes translates to being a cautious guest on our show. Some chefs need a helping hand, and it's my job to sort of guide them and nudge them forward. That's what it was like the first time Hiroshi appeared on *Hawai'i's Kitchen*. I more or less extended my hand to him and said, in effect, "Please come with me on this journey. Let's go. It'll be okay!"

The second time around, however, he was warmed up and ready to go. To me, that shows how far Hiroshi has come and the large strides he continues to make. Trust me, people who haven't heard of Hiroshi Fukui will know all about him soon enough. He's working hard and making a name for himself every single day.

Pan-Seared Jumbo Sea Scallops

4   sea scallops (10-count size), cleaned
            salt and pepper, to taste
2 tbsp.   vegetable oil

Bacon Takana Ragout
1 tbsp.   olive oil
1 tbsp.   finely diced bacon
1 tbsp.   finely diced onion
1/2 tbsp.   finely minced garlic
1 tbsp.   takana
1 tbsp.   fresh corn kernels
1-1/2 tbsp. diced tomato

Beurre Blanc
3 tbsp.   diced onion
3/4 cup   white wine
1-1/2 cups heavy cream
1/2 lb.   cold butter, cut into small cubes
1/8 tsp.   white pepper
3/4 tsp.   salt
1/4 tsp.   light soy sauce (usukuchi)
1-tsp.   fish sauce

Onion Chive Oil
1 cup   vegetable oil
1/2 cup   roughly chopped onion chive
            salt and pepper, to taste

Teriyaki Glaze
1-1/2 cups sake
1/2 cup   dark soy sauce
1/2 cup   sugar

Pat scallops dry and season with salt and pepper. Heat pan until smoking and add oil. When the oil is smoking, add scallops. Cook 2 minutes on each side or until cooked in the center to medium. To make ragout: Heat oil to medium; add bacon. Allow bacon to flavor the oil for 2 to 3 minutes. Add onion and garlic; allow to simmer in the oil 2 more minutes. Add takana and corn. Allow the mixture to stew and heat thoroughly in the oil. Remove from heat and add tomatoes. Set aside. To make beurre blanc: Place onions and wine in a pot and reduce by 3/4. Add cream; reduce by one-third. Stir in butter a little at a time. Season with remaining ingredients; strain.To make chive oil: Combine ingredients and blend until smooth. To make glaze: Combine ingredients and cook over low heat until the mixture reduces enough to coat the back of a spoon. Extra glaze may be refrigerated for several weeks. To plate each dish: Place a spoonful of ragout on plate, top with 1 scallop. Drizzle beurre blanc around plate. Drizzle with chive oil and teriyaki glaze. Note: Takana is a Japanese salted, seasoned mustard cabbage. It may be found in Japanese markets under the names takana abura itame or takana kasu. Do not substitute the Chinese version of sour mustard cabbage or pickled cabbage.

Garlic Shichimi 'Ahi with Ponzu Vinaigrette

1 lb.	'ahi fillet
2 tbsp.	minced garlic
1/2 tsp.	salt
1/2 cup	shichimi (Japanese 7-spice mix)
2 tbsp.	grated daikon radish
1/2 tsp.	momiji oroshi (Japanese chili paste)
1 tbsp.	minced onion chive
1/2	vine-ripened tomato
	mixed greens
1/2 cup	ponzu sauce
1/4 cup	olive oil

Brush 'ahi with minced garlic and sprinkle salt on both sides. Roll the 'ahi in shichimi. Quickly sear in a hot skillet or under a broiler. The inside should be rare. Thinly slice 'ahi and arrange on plate, leaving the center of the plate open. Mix the daikon and momiji oroshi. Garnish each 'ahi slice with the daikon mixture and onion chive. Thinly slice the tomato and arrange in a ring in the center of the plate. Top with greens. Blend ponzu sauce and olive oil. Pour around the edge of the 'ahi. Serves 4.

Sizzlin' Moi Carpaccio

1	whole moi, about 12 oz., filleted and skinned
1/8 tsp.	salt
1/8 tsp.	cracked pepper
1 tsp.	minced garlic
2 tbsp.	finely diced soft tofu
2 tbsp.	finely julienned ginger
2 tbsp.	finely diced tomato, skin only
2 tbsp.	onion chive or green onion in 1/2-inch lengths
4 tbsp.	peanut oil
1/2 tsp.	sesame oil
2 tsp.	thinly sliced nori kizami
8 tbsp.	prepared ponzu sauce

Slice moi into paper-thin slices and divide among four plates, fanning the pieces in a circle. Sprinkle with salt and pepper; brush with garlic. Divide the next four ingredients among the plates, layering them as follows: tofu, ginger, tomato, and chives. Combine oils in a saucepan and heat until smoking. Pour over the fish as the oil sizzles. Top each serving with nori and drizzle 2 tbsp. of ponzu around each plate. Serves 4.

Soy Steamed Veal Cheek with Asian Succotash and Yellow Mustard Aioli

10 pieces	veal cheek (4 oz. each)
	flour for dusting
1/4 cup	vegetable oil
20 oz.	water
1/2 cup	sake
1/2 cup	soy sauce
1 cup	mirin
1/2	medium onion, diced
1/2	carrot, chopped
1 stalk	celery, chopped
5 cloves	garlic
2-inch piece	ginger, smashed
2 stalks	green onion, chopped

Succotash

1/2 cup	fresh corn kernels
1/2 cup	shelled soy beans
1/2 cup	carrots, small dice, cooked
1 tbsp.	butter
	salt and pepper, to taste

Aioli

1/4 cup	mayonnaise
1 tbsp.	yellow mustard paste, or to taste
1/4 tsp.	fish sauce
1/4 tsp.	lemon juice
	salt and pepper, to taste

Dust veal cheek with flour; sear both sides in oil until golden brown. Remove and dip in hot water to remove excess oil. Place in a crock or pan. Pour water, sake, soy sauce and mirin over the cheeks and cover with cheesecloth. Place vegetables on top of cheesecloth; cover with another layer of cheesecloth. Wrap tightly with plastic wrap, making sure all the vegetables are submerged in liquid. Place the pan in a larger pot of boiling water and steam 3 to 4 hours, until fork-tender. Discard vegetables. Serves 5. To make succotash: Saute vegetables in butter until crisp-tender; season with salt and pepper. To make aioli: Mix ingredients until well-combined. Serve veal (2 pieces per serving) atop rice or mashed potatoes, surrounded by succotash and 1/4 cup of strained cooking broth. Garnish with aioli. Serves 5.
Note: Veal cheek is a specialty cut that may be difficult to obtain. Substitute veal shank (use five 1-pound pieces with bone) or beef ribeye (about 2-1/2 lbs. total, 1-inch thick, cut in 10 pieces).

Steamed Onaga with Roasted Garlic-Tomato Vinaigrette and Truffled Micro Greens

4	4-oz. onaga fillets
	salt and pepper, to taste
2 tbsp.	sake
1/4 cup	micro greens
1 tbsp.	white truffle oil

Tomato Vinaigrette

1	vine-ripened red tomato
1	vine-ripened yellow tomato
	salt, to taste
	olive oil
3	slices bacon
12 cloves	roasted garlic, peeled
1 cup	olive oil
2 tsp.	Thai fish sauce (nam pla)
1/2 tsp.	sriracha (chili sauce)
2 tbsp.	oyster sauce
1/8 tsp.	fresh cracked black pepper
1 tbsp.	lemon juice

Beurre Blanc

3 tbsp.	minced shallots
3/4 cup	white wine
1-1/2 cups	heavy whipping cream
1/2 lb.	unsalted butter
1/8 tsp.	white pepper
	salt, to taste
1 tsp.	Thai fish sauce (nam pla)
1/4 tsp.	light soy sauce

To make vinaigrette: Preheat oven to 300 degrees. Halve tomatoes, core and remove the seeds. Sprinkle lightly with salt and olive oil and roast in the oven for 10 to 15 minutes, until slightly soft (do not overcook; retain the texture of the tomato). Chop tomatoes. Cut bacon into half-inch squares and slowly cook in 1/2 cup olive oil until cooked but not crispy. Cook garlic cloves in remaining 1/2 cup olive oil until soft and lightly browned. Strain both oils and set aside. Mince enough garlic cloves to make 3 tablespoons. Combine the remaining vinaigrette ingredients plus salt (optional) with the minced roasted garlic, 4 tbsp. bacon oil and 6 tbsp. garlic oil. Pour over the chopped tomatoes. To make beurre blanc: Reduce shallots and wine in a non-reactive pot until just 2 tablespoons are left. Add heavy cream and reduce by 1/3, then remove from the heat and add butter a little at a time. Add the remaining seasonings and strain. Keep in a warm place. To prepare the fish: Place onaga in a pan and season with salt and pepper. Pour sake over fish and steam until done, 6 to 8 minutes. Ladle about 2 tablespoons of the beurre blanc on each of 4 plates. Top the sauce with a fillet. Drizzle Tomato Vinaigrette around the fish. Top each fillet with micro greens and drizzle the greens with truffle oil. Serves 4.

Agedashi Tofu

1-1/4 cups	dashi (below)
1/4 cup	light soy sauce
1/4 cup	mirin
1 block	soft tofu
1/2 cup	potato starch
4 cups	vegetable oil

Garnish

2 tbsp.	grated daikon
2 tbsp.	ginger
2 tbsp.	sliced green onions
1 tbsp.	ume purée

Bring dashi, shoyu and mirin to a boil; remove from heat. Heat oil to 360 degrees. Cut tofu into 8 blocks and coat lightly in potato starch. Deep fry 4-6 minutes until outside is crispy. Place tofu blocks side-by-side in 4 bowls and garnish with daikon, ginger, green onions and ume purée. Pour sauce from the side halfway up each tofu block. Serves 4.

Dashi

4 cups	water
1 pc.	konbu (2 in. square)
handful	bonito flakes

Heat water and konbu in a pot. Just before the water boils (you'll see small bubbles coming out of the konbu), remove the konbu. Allow water to come to a full boil, then add bonito and immediately remove from heat. Let sit for a minute or so; strain.

Beverly Gannon

HALI'IMAILE
GENERAL STORE

How did Beverly Gannon go from being a road manager for some of the biggest names in show business — including Liza Minnelli and Ben Vereen — to becoming one of Hawai'i's most talented and respected chefs? I'm not exactly sure, but my taste buds and I are glad she did.

Anyone who's eaten at Hali'imaile General Store or Joe's Bar & Grill on Maui knows about Bev's incredible food and the fresh Island ingredients that help define her style of Hawai'i Regional Cuisine. (She's one of the group's 12 founding members, along with Sam Choy, Roy Yamaguchi, George Mavrothalassitis, Alan Wong and the rest). Today, she and her husband, Joe (that's him with Bev on page 39), are like the Duchess and Duke of Hāli'imaile — they're like culinary royalty over there!

But they don't act like it. They're such nice, unassuming people, and I'm glad to call them dear friends.

Talk about dedication. Bev gave up her career in the entertainment industry because she simply loved to cook. She attended the prestigious Le Cordon Bleu in London and also learned from top chefs in Italy and France. A native of Dallas, she returned home to work as a caterer before starting a catering company of her own in 1980. It was then that she met Joe, who was himself an entertainment producer and director. The two moved to Maui, got married and opened another catering business. In 1987, they opened Hali'imaile General Store at the old store site in upcountry Maui. Eight years later, they opened Joe's Bar & Grill in Wailea.

She's been one busy lady ever since. In fact, I only recently found out that Bev has been working with Hawaiian Airlines as its executive chef since 1999.

Bev has been on *Hawai'i's Kitchen* several times. I love it when she's a guest, because all I have to do is introduce her and then step back. After that, it becomes her show, and I'm the guest! Her personality just takes over. In fact, even though I'm the host of the show, sometimes I feel like I'm just visiting her at home.

Lemongrass Prawn Soup

Broth

2-1/2 lbs.	whitefish bones, i.e., mahimahi, opakapaka, hapu'upu'u (not salmon)
18	(16/20 per-pound count) shrimp, peeled and deveined; reserve shells
1 tbsp.	olive oil
1 cup	Maui onions, peeled and coarsely chopped
6	garlic cloves
1 tbsp.	ginger, peeled and coarsely chopped
2 stalks	lemongrass, peeled, split, smashed and coarsely chopped
8	ripe plum tomatoes, quartered
1 tsp.	salt
1 tsp.	whole black peppercorns
1 tsp.	Szechuan peppercorns
1 tsp.	coriander seeds
1 cup	white wine
2 qts.	water

Preheat oven to 400 degrees. Rinse the fish bones and shrimp shells well and drain. Place on a cookie sheet and roast for 15 minutes. Remove from the oven and set aside. In a 4-quart pot over medium-high heat, add the olive oil. Add the onions, garlic, ginger and lemongrass; stir for 2 minutes. Add fish bones and shrimp shells. Stir for 3 to 4 minutes. Add tomatoes, followed by the rest of the ingredients. Increase heat and bring to a boil. Reduce heat and simmer, uncovered, for 2 hours. Remove pot from the heat and strain soup through cheesecloth twice, pressing on the bones and shells to remove all the juices. Taste and adjust seasoning. (Soup broth may be prepared in advance and kept refrigerated.)

Soup (ingredients per person)
1 qt.   water
1 cup   white wine
3   shrimp
5   haricot vert or green beans
3   asparagus tips
1   shiitake mushroom, stem removed
            bowl of ice water

Garnish
1 sprig   cilantro
2 wedges   vine-ripened tomato

In a 2-quart saucepan over high heat, bring water and wine
to a boil. Reduce heat to a simmer. Add shrimp and simmer
2 minutes, until cooked. Remove and set aside. Add beans,
asparagus and mushroom and simmer for 60 seconds.
Remove to the ice-water bath to stop cooking. Drain and
set aside. To assemble, place the soup ingredients in individual bowls. Add hot broth (opposite), garnish with tomato
wedges and cilantro sprig and serve immediately.

Chicken Curry

1/2 cup	unsalted butter
2	large onions, finely sliced
3	carrots, peeled and bias cut into 1/4-in. thick pieces
4 stalks	celery, peeled and bias cut into 1/4-in. thick slices
2	large Granny Smith apples, peeled, cut into 1/4-in. thick slices
2 tbsp.	curry powder
1/2 cup	flour
1-1/2 cups	chicken stock
1-1/2 cups	coconut milk
1 cup	heavy cream
3 to 4 cups	cooked chicken, cut into large dices

Melt the butter in a large saute pan over medium heat. Add onions, celery and carrots and saute for 3 to 4 minutes until the vegetables begin to wilt. Add apples. Saute 2 minutes. Add curry powder and stir until well-blended. Add flour and stir until well-blended. Cook another 3 to 4 minutes. Add chicken stock, coconut milk and cream. Stir until thickened. Add chicken. Serve with jasmine rice and little bowls of condiments, such as dried cranberries, cashews, macadamia nuts, chopped green onions, mandarin oranges, diced crisp bacon, toasted coconut, raisins, assorted bottled chutneys or green stuffed olives. Serves 8.

Pork Chops With Mustard Sauce

6	pork chops (1-1/2 inches thick)
	salt and pepper, to taste
	flour, for dredging
2 tbsp.	unsalted butter
3 tbsp.	olive oil
1-1/2 cups	thinly sliced onions
3 tbsp.	white balsamic vinegar
3 tbsp.	rich chicken stock

Mustard Sauce

3/4 cup	whipping cream
2 tsp.	dijon mustard
1 tbsp.	lemon juice
	fresh thyme, to taste

Preheat oven to 325 degrees. Season the pork chops with salt and pepper, then dredge in flour. Melt the butter and oil in a skillet and brown the chops on both sides. Place in a heavy casserole. Remove all but 2 tbsp. of the pork chop drippings from the skillet. Add the onions and saute until nicely browned. Add the vinegar, then the chicken stock. Bring to a boil and deglaze the pan. Pour over the chops. Bake until cooked through. Remove the chops and keep warm. To make the sauce: Remove excess fat from the casserole (if the casserole is not stovetop-safe, transfer the drippings to a skillet). Add cream. Heat on top of the stove until the sauce thickens. Add mustard, then lemon juice and thyme. Strain the sauce and serve over the pork chops.

Macadamia Nut Crusted Mahimahi with Mango Hollandaise

1 cup	macadamia nuts
1 cup	panko
1/2 cup	fresh cilantro
1/2 cup	mayonnaise
2 tsp.	sambal chili paste
6	6-oz. mahimahi fillets
	salt and pepper, to taste
	canola olive oil blend

To prepare the coating: Place nuts, panko and cilantro in a food processor and process until fine. Spread on plate. In a bowl, combine the mayonnaise and chili paste. Season fish with salt and pepper. Evenly spread a light coat of chili mayonnaise on one side of the fish fillet. Coat the same side evenly with the breading. In a saute pan, pour enough oil to cover bottom of pan and heat over medium heat. Add the fish, crust side down, and saute for 3 minutes or until golden brown. Turn fish and cook another 3 minutes. Remove to plate and sauce with Mango Hollandaise.

Mango Hollandaise

1/4 cup	vinegar
1/2	shallot, peeled and chopped
1 tsp.	finely chopped lemongrass
3	egg yolks
1/8	scant tsp. cayenne
2 tbsp.	mango purée
1/2 lb.	melted butter
1/2 tsp.	salt, or to taste

In a small saucepan, combine vinegar, shallot and lemon-grass and reduce to 1 tbsp. Place in a blender. Add the egg yolks and cayenne, followed by the mango purée. With the blender running, slowly add butter. Season with salt. The best way to keep a butter sauce warm is to place it in a thermos. The sauce will remain at the correct temperature for several hours without breaking the container.

Pork Loin with Dried Fruit

6	dried pears
12	dried prunes
12	dried apricots
1/2 cup	apple juice
1/2 cup	water
2-1/2 lbs.	pork loin, cut into fillets
	salt and pepper, to taste
2 tbsp.	unsalted butter
1 tbsp.	olive oil
3	shallots, chopped
1/2 cup	rich chicken stock

Sauce
1-1/2 tbsp.	calvados (apple brandy)
1 cup	heavy whipping cream
1 tbsp.	lemon juice

Place the dried fruit in a saucepan. Cover with apple juice and water. Bring to a boil, then reduce heat and simmer until tender (timing varies). Strain. Preheat oven to 325 degrees. Season the pork with salt and pepper. Heat the butter and oil in a heavy saute pan. Add the pork fillets and saute until golden brown. Add the shallots and stock. Cover and cook until the fillets are cooked through. Remove to a platter and keep warm. To make the sauce: Remove any excess fat from the skillet. Add the calvados and cream. Reduce until thickened. Add lemon juice. Adjust seasonings and strain. Garnish with dried fruit compote.

Portuguese Steamed Clams

1 tbsp.	finely chopped garlic
2 cups	chopped onion
3 cups	chopped red bell pepper
1/3 cup	olive oil
1/2 lb.	mild Portuguese sausage in 1/4-in. chunks
1-1/2 cups	sake
6 cups	rich fish stock or canned clam juice
2 tbsp.	chili sauce
2 cups	peeled, seeded and coarsely diced tomatoes
5 dozen	clams
1/2 cup	chopped cilantro

In a large pan, saute garlic, onions and red pepper in olive oil for 2 minutes. Add the sausage. Cook another 5 minutes. Add sake and deglaze the pan. Add the fish stock and reduce by half. Add the chili sauce and tomatoes. Add the clams; cover and cook until the clams open, 6 to 8 minutes. Ladle into bowls and garnish with cilantro. Serves 6.

Chocolate Chip Cookie Pie

3/4 cup	light brown sugar, packed
1/2 cup	flour
1/2 tsp.	baking powder
1/4 tsp.	ground cinnamon
2	eggs, slightly beaten
1 cup	Hershey's semi-sweet or milk-chocolate chips
1 cup	walnuts, toasted and coarsely chopped
9 in.	pie crust, baked and cooled

Preheat oven to 350 degrees. In a bowl stir together brown sugar, flour, baking powder and cinnamon. Add eggs, stirring until well-blended. Stir in chocolate chips and walnuts. Pour into the pie crust. Bake about 30 to 35 minutes until lightly browned and set. Serve with vanilla bean ice cream.

D.K. Kodama

Seafood Restaurant
& Sushi Bar

DK. Kodama is one of the most personable guys you'll ever meet. He's just a lovable teddy bear of a guy. And he laughs at everything! *"Hey, D.K., how you doing?"* Ho, he's cracking up already!

I'll tell you a little secret about how I do *Hawai'i's Kitchen.* You can actually feel the personality of the chef before we even start taping the show. I'll come in, meet the chef and talk story with him. By the time the show starts, I know what to expect from him. If he's good to

go, I step back a little, give him the space that he needs and only jump in when I need to.

D.K. is one of those guys. In fact, I think he has the kind of personality that would enable him to host his own show some day. He's got an aura about him, and I love his sense of humor!

D.K. was born and raised on O'ahu, and he actually planned to follow in his father's footsteps as a civil engineer before he caught the cooking bug. He spent more than a decade in Seattle, Aspen and other locales throughout the U.S., Mexico and the Caribbean. He soaked up a whole new world of flavors and culinary styles, all the while learning the fine art of sushi making.

He returned to the Islands and opened Sansei Seafood Restaurant & Sushi Bar at the Kapalua resort in 1996. Four years after that, D.K. opened his Honolulu location at Restaurant Row. Both restaurants have earned high praise from the critics, including being named one  of *Bon Appétit's* Favorite Asian Restaurants and one of America's Best Sushi Bars in *Travel & Leisure*.

I can personally vouch for D.K.'s culinary skills. I tell you, this guy is black-belt sushi!

Once, D.K. and I went to Las Vegas on a promotional tour for the state of Hawai'i. We were at a reception near this sushi bar that was owned by a friend of mine. Well, when D.K. walked in, it was like all the chefs there were in awe of him. *This is D.K. Kodama of Sansei!* But he made everyone feel so comfortable, and he and the chefs wound up making sushi for all of us that night. That was very cool!

If I were into puns, I'd tell you that D.K. is one sushi chef who's definitely on a "roll." But I'm not, so I'll spare you.

Asian Paella of Shrimp and Jonah Crab with Kaffir Lime Beurre Blanc

1 tsp.	chopped shallots
1 tbsp.	chopped garlic
2-1/2 tsp.	grated ginger
1	medium onion, diced
2 stalks	celery, diced
1	medium green bell pepper, diced
2	red chilies, seeded and diced
2 tbsp.	olive oil
1-1/2 cups	Japanese rice
4	kaffir lime leaves
1 qt.	rich seafood stock
1 qt.	sake
	salt and pepper, to taste
1 cup	black turtle beans, cooked
2 lb.	shrimp (26/30 count) peeled and deveined
1 lb.	Jonah crab claws
8	Thai basil leaves, for garnish
8	fluffy bunches cilantro leaves, for garnish

Kaffir Lime Beurre Blanc

2 cups	white wine
1/2 cup	lime juice
1/2 cup	cream
1	kaffir lime leaf
2 lb.	unsalted butter at room temperature, cubed
	salt and pepper, to taste

In a deep skillet over medium high heat, cook the shallots, garlic, ginger, onion, celery, bell pepper and chilies in the olive oil until the onion is translucent. Add the rice and lime leaves and stir to mix. Pour the stock and sake over the rice and season with salt and black pepper. Reduce heat and cover. Simmer until rice is almost done, about 15 minutes. The rice should still have a slight crunch. Fold in the turtle beans. Top with shrimp and crab. Cover and remove from heat. Let stand for 10 to 15 minutes, until the shrimp are just cooked (the shrimp should be pink and slightly firm). To make the sauce: In a medium saucepan over high heat, stir the wine, lime juice and cream until reduced by 2/3. Put the mixture into a blender and blend at medium speed, adding butter one piece at a time. Season with salt and pepper. To serve: Place the rice mixture in the center of a large bowl. Top with cooked shrimp and crab and ladle sauce over the dish. Garnish with basil and cilantro.
Serves 6 to 8. Ingredient notes: Turtle beans are Cuban black beans sold dry or canned. Jonah crabs are a cousin of the Florida stone crab and can be purchased frozen. Substitute any type of crab claw.

Asian Tostada with Shichimi-Seared Opah, Shrimp and Shiso Salad and Spicy Umeboshi Vinaigrette

4 cups	cottonseed oil
4	won ton wrappers
12 oz.	opah, cut in 1/2-inch cubes
	salt and pepper, to taste
	shichimi (Japanese 7-pepper spice), to taste
6	shrimp (16/20 count size), cooked and chopped
3	fresh, ripe tomatoes, cut into 1/2-inch cubes
2	Japanese cucumbers, cut into 1/4-inch cubes
12	shiso leaves, julienned
2 cups	mesclun greens
	Spicy Umeboshi Vinaigrette
1 tsp.	sesame seeds
1 oz.	masago or tobiko caviar

Heat oil to 350 degrees. Fry won ton wrappers, keeping them flat, until crisp and golden, about 4 minutes. Season opah with salt, pepper and shichimi. Sear or roast to medium doneness, about 2 minutes. Combine opah with shrimp, tomatoes and cucumbers. Just before serving, mix in the shiso leaves. To serve: Divide greens among 4 plates. Place a won ton wrapper on each pile of greens. Top won ton wrapper with the opah and shrimp mixture. Drizzle with Spicy Umeboshi Vinaigrette. Sprinkle with sesame seeds and caviar. Serves 4.

Spicy Umeboshi Vinaigrette

2 cups	vegetable oil
1/2 tsp.	chopped garlic
2 tsp.	ume paste
1/2 tsp.	chopped shallots
1 tsp.	sugar
1/4 cup	rice wine vinegar
dash	white pepper
1 tsp.	dry mustard
dash	soy sauce
1/2 tsp.	liquid from jar of ume
dash	dashi

Blend together oil, garlic, ume paste, shallots and sugar. Add remaining ingredients and mix well. Note: Ume is a Japanese pickled plum. To make ume paste, remove seeds from a few ume and mash.

Braised Veal Shanks with Rosemary and Thyme Essence

4	veal shanks, 3-inches each
	salt and freshly ground black pepper, to taste
1 cup	flour
2 tbsp.	olive oil
1/2 cup	minced garlic
1 cup	chopped celery
1 cup	chopped carrots
1 cup	coarsely chopped onion
1 cup	chopped leeks (white part only)
1 tbsp.	fresh rosemary, plus 4 sprigs for garnish
1 tbsp.	fresh thyme, plus 4 sprigs for garnish
1 cup	red wine (cabernet or merlot)
1/2 gallon	veal stock (1 46-ounce can of beef broth)
2 tbsp.	butter, at room temperature

Preheat oven to 375 degrees. Season the veal shanks with salt and pepper, then dredge in flour. In a thick-bottomed skillet over medium-high heat, brown the shanks in the oil an all sides, about 5 minutes. Reduce heat to medium. Add garlic and cook until translucent, about 2 minutes. Add celery, carrots, onions, leeks and herbs, and cook until just tender, about 5 more minutes. Deglaze the pan with wine and stock. Place the browned shanks in a deep, oven-proof casserole dish and pour the garlic and vegetable mixture on top of the shanks. Cover and roast in the oven for 1-1/2 to 2 hours. The meat should be moist and fork-tender, almost ready to fall off of the bone. Remove the shanks and keep warm. Strain pan juices and reduce by 1/2 over medium-high heat. Add the butter and stir until smooth. Pour the sauce over the shanks. Garnish with thyme and rosemary sprigs. Serve with marrow forks to get to the rich marrow inside the bone. Serves 4.

Fresh Corn Polenta with King Crab Legs and Wild Mushroom Ragout

8 ears	corn
2 tbsp.	heavy cream
4 tbsp.	unsalted butter
	kosher salt and freshly ground black pepper, to taste
1 tbsp.	minced garlic
1 cup	quartered shiitake mushrooms
1 cup	quartered white mushrooms
1 cup	demi-glaze (homemade or store-bought)
4	king crab legs, maris cut (cut crosswise and lengthwise)
1/2 cup	micro arugula or any small, leafy baby herb, for garnish

Score the corn vertically with a knife. Run the back of the knife edge along the scored kernels to extract the corn milk and pulp. In a medium saucepan over medium heat, simmer corn milk and pulp for about 10 minutes, until thickened to the consistency of a soft polenta. Add the cream and reduce the heat to low for 5 more minutes. Fold in 2 tbsp. of the butter until smooth and well-incorporated. Season with salt and pepper. Keep warm. In a medium skillet over medium-high heat, melt 1 tbsp. of butter and cook the garlic until soft (do not overcook or garlic will be bitter). Add the mushrooms and saute for 5 more minutes until the mushrooms are cooked. Add the demi-glaze and simmer five more minutes. Keep warm. In another large skillet over medium high-heat, melt 1 tbsp. butter and add the crab. Heat until just warmed, about 7 minutes. To serve: Spoon polenta mixture into the center of the plate and top with mushroom ragout. Top the ragout with crab legs. Garnish with the micro arugula and serve hot. Serves 4.

Goat Cheese and Wild Mushroom Ravioli with Balsamic Syrup and Sweet Shoyu

1-1/2 cups wild mushrooms (i.e., shiitake or oyster)
1/4 cup   Maui onion, diced
4 tbsp.   goat cheese, crumbled
1/2 tsp.   fresh thyme leaves
1 tsp.   minced garlic
            salt and freshly ground pepper, to taste
12   won ton or gyoza wrappers (2 inches square)
1/2 cup   reduced balsamic vinegar
1/2 cup   sweet soy sauce

Saute mushrooms over medium heat about 3 minutes. Add onions and saute until mushrooms are tender and onions are translucent, about 2 more minutes. Cool. Combine onions and mushrooms with goat cheese. Season with herbs, garlic, salt and pepper. Place a won ton wrapper on a clean, dry surface. Place 1 tbsp. of the onion and mushroom mixture in the center of the wrapper. Brush the edges of the wrapper with water and fold in half diagonally. Press down to squeeze out any air. Press on the edges to seal. Repeat with the remaining wrappers and filling. Cover and refrigerate the ravioli for about 1 hour. Poach in simmering water about 3 minutes, until tender. Drain. Place on a serving plate. Drizzle with vinegar and sweet soy sauce. Serves 4. Note: Reduced balsamic vinegar may be found in specialty food stores. Sweet soy sauce, also called kecap manis, may be found in Asian markets.

Spring Vegetable Risotto with Morel Mushrooms and Waialua Asparagus

2 tbsp.	vegetable oil
1 cup	diced Maui onion
1 cup	morel mushrooms or any wild mushroom, sliced
2 cups	Japanese rice or any short-grain rice
1 cup	plum wine
8 cups	chicken stock
1 lb.	cold butter, roughly chopped
1/2 cup	roughly chopped asparagus, blanched
1/2 cup	halved grape tomatoes
	salt and pepper, to taste
	freshly grated Asiago cheese
1	black truffle, shaved (optional)

Heat the oil in a medium saucepot on medium-high heat. Add the onions and cook until translucent, about 2 minutes. Add the mushrooms and saute for 3 minutes. Add the rice and continue to saute for 2 minutes. De-glaze the pot with plum wine and cook for 1 minute. Add 2 cups of stock and reduce the heat to low. Simmer until the liquid is absorbed. Add the rest of the stock, 1 cup at a time, and the butter, 4 oz. at a time, allowing the liquid to absorb between additions. Fold the asparagus and the tomatoes into the risotto and season with salt and pepper. Divide the risotto among 4 to 6 bowls and sprinkle with grated cheese and truffle slices. Serves 4 to 6.

Seafood Cannelloni with Masago Aioli and Ogo Salad

4	large russet potatoes, peeled, sliced very thin and blanched
1 cup	cooked crab meat, squeezed dry
1 cup	cooked shrimp, squeezed dry
2 tbsp.	chopped green onion
2 tbsp.	chopped fresh basil
2 tbsp.	finely diced celery
3 cups	cottonseed oil

Masago Aioli

5 cloves	garlic
5	extra large egg yolks
5 tsp.	fresh lemon juice
1-3/4 cups	olive oil
dash	coarse salt
dash	cayenne pepper
1/8 cup	masago (smelt roe)

Ogo Salad

5 cups	fresh ogo
1/2 cup	thinly sliced Maui onion
2 tsp.	coarse salt
1/4 cup	chopped green onion
1/2 tbsp.	sugar
1/4 cup	rice wine vinegar
1/2 tsp.	minced fresh ginger
3 tbsp.	soy sauce

To make Ogo Salad: Blanch the ogo in boiling water. Drain and cut into small pieces. Combine with the remaining salad ingredients and chill for 2 hours.To make Masago Aioli: In a blender at medium speed, combine the garlic, yolks and lemon juice until smooth, about 2 minutes. Add the oil gradually until the mixture thickens. Season with salt and cayenne pepper. Fold in the masago. Refrigerate until needed. To make the cannelloni: Overlap two potato slices to form a 4-by-6-inch rectangle. Combine the remaining ingredients and form a spoonful into a hot dog shape on the potato slices. Roll the potato around the mixture to form the cannelloni. Repeat with remaining potato slices and filling. Heat oil to 350 degrees. Pan-fry the cannelloni for about 5 minutes or until golden brown. Pat dry. To serve: Place two cannelloni in the center of each plate. Drizzle with Masago Aioli and top with the Ogo Salad. Garnish with more chopped green onions and white sesame seeds. Serves 10.

Tempura-Fried Nori Wrapped Scallop Mousse with Wasabi Cream

1 lb.	scallops
2	eggs
1/4 cup	cream
	salt and pepper, to taste
4	sheets nori
	flour, for dredging
2 cups	tempura batter
4 cups	cottonseed oil for frying

Sauce

4 tbsp.	wasabi powder
5 tbsp.	water
1 tsp.	mirin
1/4 cup	cream

Place the scallops in a food processor and process until smooth. Add the eggs and cream. Process again until light and fluffy. Season with salt and pepper. Chill. Place 2 to 3 tbsp. of the scallop mousse on each sheet of nori, near the bottom edge. Roll up firmly but not so tight that the filling comes out the sides. Seal with a little water. Chill. Heat oil to 350 degrees. Dredge the rolls in flour, then dip in tempura batter. Fry until firm, 3 to 4 minutes. Drain on a wire rack or paper towel for 2 to 3 minutes. Slice each roll into 5 pieces and place on a serving plate. To make the sauce: Mix the wasabi powder with the water to make a slurry. Add the mirin and cream. Mix until smooth, then adjust the flavor by adding more cream or mirin, if needed. Drizzle over rolls before serving. Serves 4. Note: If you use frozen scallops, be sure to thaw and dry them completely to remove excess moisture. Purchase a commercial tempura batter mix and prepare according to package directions.

George Mavrothalassitis

chef *Mavro*

y role on *Hawai'i's Kitchen* is strictly one of facilitator. I'm just the guy through whom the audience can experience the show vicariously.

To be honest, the average viewer probably knows more about cooking than I do. So on the show, I ask a lot of questions: "What was that you just threw in the pot?" "Why did you add that?" "Can you explain the process for me?"

Whenever Chef Mavro is our guest, however, the rules change a bit. With his heavy French accent and hyper personality, sometimes I can't

understand a word he says. I mean, with Mavro, I need English subtitles! *Slow down! Take it easy, Mavro!*

But this guy is great. He's done it all. George Mavrothalassitis was born in France, near the old port of Marseilles. He learned from some of the masters of contemporary French cooking before opening Restaurant Mavro in Marseilles and Restaurant La Presquile in Cassis. Mavro joined the Halekulani in 1988, helping La Mer become Hawai'i's only AAA Five Diamond restaurant in 1992. Before opening his O'ahu restaurant in 1998, he served as senior executive chef at the Four Seasons Resort Maui at Wailea and chef de cuisine of that hotel's Seasons restaurant. In May 2003, Mavro earned the prestigious James Beard Best Chef award for the Pacific Northwest/ Hawai'i region.

Mavro just exudes energy. He's an enjoyable guy to be around, and while you'd think his accent might pose a problem when he appears on our show, I think it actually enhances the program. It adds an element of fun.

I'll tell you something about Mavro, though. He has a secret weapon: His wife, Donna Jung. Donna will make sure that he has the best possible environ-ment that he needs to work in. Of course, all the chefs we feature are professionals, and they could probably perform under less-than-standard conditions. But it's  important to have someone like Donna who can provide him the means to do the very best.

Mavro and Donna make a great team, and I absolutely love Mavro's restaurant. If I could only understand what he's saying!

Coriander Crusted Beef Strip Loin with Pinot Noir-Anchovy Essence, Olive Oil-Caper Mashed Potatoes and Waimea Tomatoes

1 lb.	beef strip loin
1 tbsp.	coriander seeds
1 tbsp.	Hawaiian salt
1 tbsp.	black pepper, whole
2 tbsp.	extra virgin olive oil
2	vine-ripened tomatoes
2 cloves	chopped garlic
1 tsp.	fresh thyme
2 tbsp.	extra virgin olive oil
	salt and pepper to taste
1/2	medium Maui onion, finely sliced
4 tbsp.	water
1/2 bottle	pinot noir
1	medium carrot
3	salted anchovy fillets, rinsed
2	large russet potatoes
1/2 cup	hot milk
1/2 cup	extra virgin olive oil
2 tbsp.	capers

To prepare the tomatoes: Peel, half and marinate them in garlic, thyme, oil, salt and pepper. Bake at 140 degrees for 12 hours. For the beef: Preheat oven to 350 degrees. Combine the coriander, Hawaiian salt and pepper. Crust each side of the strip loin with the spice mixture. Heat the oil in a pan over medium heat; saute beef for 8 minutes per side. Finish the beef in the oven, roasting to desired doneness. Allow the meat to rest 10 minutes before slicing. For the sauce: Cut the carrot into pieces and boil 15 minutes. Simmer the onions in the water until translucent. Divide the wine into three parts. Add 1/3 to the onions and cook until the liquid is evaporated. Repeat with the second 1/3 of the wine. Add the last 1/3 of the wine and reduce by half. Place in a blender with the cooked carrot and anchovy. Blend until very smooth; strain. Salt and pepper to taste. For the mashed potatoes: Boil them in their skins for 35 minutes. Peel and mash the potatoes, preferably through a vegetable mill. Stir in the hot milk and olive oil. Garnish with the capers. To serve, slice the beef into medallions. Spoon some sauce onto each serving plate, then top with the beef slices. Surround with the tomatoes and mashed potatoes. Serves 2.

Roasted "Maple Leaf" Duck with Chinese Five-Spice Citrus Sauce and Almond, Mango and Frisee Salad

2	whole ducks
1 tbsp.	red Hawaiian salt
	white pepper, to taste
1/2 cup	sugar
1/2 cup	lemon juice
1 cup	veal demi-glace
1/4 tbsp.	Chinese five-spice
1	mango, peeled and julienned
1	head curly endive, white part only
1 tbsp.	sliced almonds
1 tbsp.	sherry vinaigrette

Preheat oven to 375 degrees. Rub the ducks inside and out with Hawaiian salt and pepper. Bake for 25 minutes. Allow the ducks to rest for 8 minutes in a warm area. Remove the breasts and set aside in a warm area. The breasts will be medium rare, but the legs will be under-cooked, so return the legs to the oven for 12 more minutes. Remove the meat from the legs and slice into very fine strips; set aside with the breasts. To prepare the sauce, simmer sugar in the lemon juice until it turns a light brown caramel color. Add the demi-glace and five-spice. Simmer for 8 minutes and salt and pepper to taste. For the salad: Combine mango with the endive, almonds and the sliced duck meat from the legs. Toss with the vinaigrette. To serve, slice the breasts into thin medallions and arrange in a circle around each serving plate. Place the salad in the center. Surround the medallions with sauce. Serves 4.

Rotisserie Island Chicken with Creamed Corn, Braised Swiss Chard and Huli-Huli Style Sauce

1	roasting chicken, preferably fresh, locally grown
1/2 cup	Huli-Huli sauce
1 tbsp.	Hawaiian salt
	pepper, to taste
1 tsp.	chopped garlic
1 tbsp.	butter
	kernels from 2 ears corn
1/2 cup	milk
1 bunch	Swiss chard
	olive oil, for sauteeing
1 tsp.	minced shallot
1 tsp.	cracked black pepper
1 tsp.	chopped garlic
1 tsp.	chopped ginger
1 cup	plum wine
1/2 cup	Huli-Huli sauce
1/2 cup	demi-glace
1	Hawaiian chili pepper
1 tsp.	sesame oil

Preheat oven to 375 degrees. Brush the chicken with Huli-Huli brand sauce and season with Hawaiian salt and pepper. Hang in the oven with rack and hook (if no rotisserie) and roast 1 hour, brushing occasionally with Huli-Huli sauce. For corn: Saute the garlic in butter. Add the corn and saute until translucent. Add the milk and simmer for 10 minutes. Place half of the cooked corn in a blender and blend until smooth. Mix in the rest of the corn. Stir in a bit more butter and season to taste. For the chard: Blanch the Swiss chard in salted boiling water; drain. Saute in olive oil, then season to taste. For the sauce: Saute the shallot, pepper, garlic and ginger. Add the plum wine. Cook until the liquid is evaporated. Add 1/2 cup Huli-Huli sauce, demiglace and chili (smashed, remove before serving). Stir in the sesame oil. Remove from heat and strain. To serve, remove the breasts and legs of the chicken. Spoon creamed corn onto 2 serving plates. Top with 1 breast and 1 leg each. Place chard in the center. Surround with sauce. Serves 2.

Grilled Keāhole Lobster with Island Watercress, Moloka'i Sweet Potato Purée and Hawaiian Vanilla Accents

1	whole, live lobster (1-1/2 lbs.)
1 quart	nage (half vegetable broth, half white wine)
2 tbsp.	olive oil
	salt and pepper, to taste
1	large sweet potato
1	Hawaiian vanilla bean pod
1 cup	milk
	butter, to taste
1	medium ripe mango, peeled, seeded and cut into pieces
2 tbsp.	mineral water
1 tsp.	sherry vinegar
1 tbsp.	vegetable oil
	salt, pepper and sugar, to taste (depending on the ripeness and sweetness of the mango)
4 sprigs	watercress
2 tbsp.	lemon-olive oil dressing (combine lemon juice, extra virgin olive oil, salt and pepper)

To prepare the lobster, poach in the nage for 8 minutes. Remove the shell from the claws and knuckles. Leave the shell on the tail, but cut in half lengthwise. Season the lobster with olive oil, salt and pepper. Grill the lobster pieces a few minutes just before serving. For the sweet potato purée, reheat oven to 450 degrees. Bake the potato 40 minutes. Peel and mash the potato, preferably by running it through a food mill. Halve the vanilla bean and scrape out the seeds. Heat the milk and add the vanilla seeds; let infuse. Combine the sweet potato with the hot milk mixture and finish with butter. To make the mango sauce, blend the ingredients together. To serve, spoon Sweet Potato Purée onto each serving plate. Surround with the mango sauce. Arrange the lobster tail, claw and knuckles on top of the purée. Top with watercress tossed with the dressing. Serves 2.

Papillote of Kūmū Baked in Parchment Paper with Seaweed and Shiitake Mushrooms

2 tbsp.	olive oil
2 tbsp.	Maui onions, finely sliced
1 6-oz.	kūmū (goatfish) fillet, with skin on, sliced into 1-inch medallions
2	medium shiitake mushrooms, sliced
1 tbsp.	basil, thinly sliced
1 sprig	red ogo
1/3 cup	white wine
1	egg yolk, beaten

Preheat oven to 375 degrees. Saute the onions in a tablespoon of olive oil until translucent. Fold a piece of parchment paper in half. Place the onions in the center of one half of the parchment paper. Top with the kumu fillet. Arrange the mushrooms over the fish, then the basil and the ogo. Drizzle with the wine. Season. Brush the egg yolk on the paper around the fish. Fold over the other half of the paper and seal. Roll in the edges all around to form the papillote. Place the papillote in a pan on high heat for 5 minutes. Place in the oven and bake for 8 minutes. Open the papillote by removing the top with scissors. Serve in paper. Serves 1.

Hawaiian Vanilla Tapioca with Maple Syrup Sauce and Creme Anglaise

1 qt.	milk
6-1/2 oz.	butter, divided use
5	Hawaiian vanilla bean pods, sliced lengthwise
9 oz.	tapioca
6	egg yolks, lightly beaten
5	egg whites
1-1/2 cup	sugar
2 oz.	butter, melted
1 qt.	half and half
3	vanilla bean pods, sliced long without seeds
12	egg yolks
2 cups	pure maple syrup
1 cup	simple syrup (boil 3/4 cup ea. water and sugar)

Bring the milk, 4 ounces of the butter and vanilla to a boil. Stir to melt butter. Add the tapioca and cook about 15 minutes, until soft, stirring constantly. Remove from heat and stir in the remaining 2-1/2 ounces of butter. Stir in the egg yolks. Cover with plastic wrap and cool to room temperature. Whip the egg whites to make a meringue, slowly adding 1/2 cup of sugar. Stir the meringue into the tapioca mixture. Preheat oven to 325 degrees. Brush 12 ramekins with the melted butter. Fill each with the tapioca mixture, place in a large baking pan and fill the pan with water 1/3 the height of ramekins. Bake ramekins in the bain-marie (water bath) for 25 minutes. Chill. For Creme Anglaise: Bring half and half to a boil with the vanilla bean pods. Whisk 1 cup sugar and egg yolks together to a ribbon consistency. Remove the milk from the heat and slowly incorporate the egg mixture, stirring constantly. Return to low heat for about 15 minutes, until the mixture is smooth and coats the bottom of the spoon. Strain and cool over an ice bath, stirring occasionally. For Maple Syrup Sauce: Heat the syrup in a pan and reduce by half. Stir in the simple syrup. To serve, remove the tapioca from the molds and place on individual serving plates. Surround with Creme Anglaise and top with Maple Syrup Sauce. Serves 12.

Colin Nishida

Side Street Inn

There are three reasons why Colin
Nishida was selected for this book.
The first reason is obvious: As anyone
who's eaten at Side Street Inn will tell
you, his food is just unbelievably good. (And plen-
tiful, too. I guarantee you won't go home hungry if
you eat at Colin's place.) It's no-nonsense food,
too. I mean, if you want good pork chops, this is
the place to go.

The second reason is less obvious, but no
less important: Side Street Inn is where many of
the best chefs in Hawai'i like to hang out, includ-

ing Alan Wong, Russell Siu,
Hiroshi Fukui, Philippe
Padovani and Roy
Yamaguchi. If the restaurant
is good enough for these
pros, it should be good
enough for us, right?

Colin himself makes an
interesting story. Unlike other
chefs in this book, he has no

formal training in the culinary arts. In fact, Colin
cut his teeth as a bartender at a bar that simply
served good food. He just wanted to offer bar
food, but his food kept getting better and better
and better. And then guys like Alan Wong started
showing up, and it gave Side Street Inn instant
credibility. It became known as the place where
Hawai'i's premier chefs go to have dinner or *pupu*.

How do I know all this? Well, the third reason that Colin was chosen for this book is a sentimental one: He and I grew up together at Moanalua Gardens. In fact, he lived right across the street from me. I made it a point to keep in touch with him whenever I could. I was really proud of him when I found out he had opened his own place.

One day, I took my mom down to Side Street Inn. I told her, "Eh, you gotta see what Colin's up to now." When we arrived, Colin came out and said, "Eh, aunty! Howzit going?" And then he went back to the kitchen and called up his mother. And Colin's mom came down! I tell you, it was awesome to see these two moms bonding again!

Because he's such a down-to-earth, unassuming guy, Colin isn't as polished as the other chefs when it comes to performing in front of the camera. I think that'll come with time. Besides, Colin is really a behind-the-scenes guy. He may not be the life of the party, but he's the guy who puts the whole party on!

Local Boy Salad

2 cups	Nalo greens
7 spears	Waialua asparagus, blanched
1	Hau'ula tomato, quartered
3 oz.	Hāmākua goat cheese, cut in 3 discs
1/4 cup	dressing

Toss vegetables and goat cheese together and top with dressing, or serve dressing on the side. Serves 1.

Dressing

1 cup	red wine vinegar
1 tbsp.	garlic
1 tbsp.	minced shallots
2-1/2 tsp.	sugar
	salt and pepper, to taste
2 tbsp.	dijon mustard
1/4 oz.	fresh oregano and thyme, minced
3 cups	olive oil

Combine all ingredients except oil in a blender or shaker bottle. Blend well, then slowly add oil, continuing to blend until emulsified. Refrigerate until needed.

Li Hing Moi

1 lb.	whole moi
	flour, for dusting
	salt and pepper, to taste
	vegetable or cottonseed oil, for deep-frying
2 cups	Nalo greens

Li Hing Mui Sauce

1 tbsp.	chopped shallots
1 tsp.	finely minced ginger
1 tsp.	chopped fresh garlic
1 tsp.	finely minced lemongrass
	juice of 1 lime
	juice of 1 medium lemon
1 tbsp.	vegetable oil
1 tbsp.	chili garlic paste
3/4 cup	honey
2	kaffir lime leaves, hand crushed (optional)
1 tbsp.	li hing mui powder, dissolved in 1 tbsp. water

Score and flour moi. Season with salt and pepper. In a frying pan or large saucepan, heat oil to 375 degrees. Deep-fry fish until golden brown. To prepare Li Hing Mui Sauce: Saute shallots, ginger, garlic, lemongrass and lime and lemon juice in oil. Add chili garlic paste, honey and lime leaf. Add dissolved li hing powder. Simmer for 10 to 15 minutes, then cool to room temperature. The sauce will thicken as it cools. To serve: Place fish over greens and top with Li Hing Mui Sauce. Serves 3 to 4. Note: The sauce may be refrigerated for 1 to 2 months. Bring to room temperature to serve.

Kapakahi Steak on Kim Chee, Watercress and Bean Sprout Salad

2 12-oz.	rib eye steaks (or other favorite steak)
	salt and pepper, to taste
	olive oil

Salad
1/2 cup	kim chee
1 tbsp.	olive oil
1 cup	chopped watercress (2-in. lengths)
1 cup	bean sprouts
1 tsp.	soy sauce

Sauce
2 strips	bacon, finely chopped
1 tbsp.	chopped onion
1	shallot, minced
1 tsp.	chopped garlic
2 tbsp.	chili pepper water
2 cups	beef stock, reduced by 2/3
1 tbsp.	Worcestershire sauce
1 tbsp.	tomato paste
	sugar, to taste
3 tbsp.	balsamic vinegar
2 tbsp.	unsalted butter

Season steaks with salt and pepper, then pan-fry in oil to desired doneness. Remove steaks from pan. To prepare the sauce: In the same pan used to cook the steaks, saute the bacon, onions, shallots and chopped garlic. Drain fat. Deglaze the pan with chili pepper water. Add reduced beef stock and bring to a simmer. Add Worcestershire sauce, tomato paste, sugar and balsamic vinegar; cook until tomato paste dissolves. Stir in butter. To prepare the salad: Saute kim chee in olive oil for 1 to 2 minutes. Add the watercress and bean sprouts and saute until wilted. Stir in soy sauce. To serve: Slice steak or serve whole atop kim chee salad. Top with sauce. Garnish with fresh watercress. Serves 4.

Side Street Inn's Fried Rice

4 cups	cooked medium-grain rice
1/2 cup	diced Portuguese sausage
2	slices bacon, diced
1/2 cup	chopped green onions
1/2 cup	frozen peas and carrots, thawed
1/2 cup	chopped char siu
4 tbsp.	oyster sauce
1 tsp.	salt
2 tbsp.	hon dashi

Chill rice in the refrigerator to dry it out, or place in the freezer for 2 hours. Brown sausage and bacon in a large skillet. Add rice and mix well. Add onions, peas, carrots and char siu; mix. Add oyster sauce, salt and hon dashi. Serves 4. Note: This dish may be adapted to whatever is available in your kitchen — leftover Spam, for instance, or lup cheong. Those sensitive to MSG may substitute a type of saimin or shrimp dashi that does not include MSG for the hon dashi and omit the salt.

Side Street's Inn-Famous Pork Chops

2 tbsp.   garlic salt
2 tbsp.   black pepper
1-1/3 cup   flour
2/3 cup   cornstarch
4   island pork chops, 7 oz. each,
            about 1-1/2 inches thick
1 cup   cottonseed or vegetable oil

Combine garlic salt, pepper, flour and cornstarch. Coat chops well in the mixture. Heat oil in a skillet. Fry chops about 10 minutes, turning frequently until browned. Cut meat from the bones and slice into bite-sized pieces. Serve over shredded cabbage with ketchup on the side. Serves 4.

Russell Siu

I f the chefs who've appeared on *Hawai'i's Kitchen* were cartoon characters, Russell Siu would definitely be the Tasmanian Devil. I mean, this guy is a study in perpetual motion!

On our set, Russell is always moving, always checking — always making sure that everything's in place. Whizzz! With him, there is no halfway. It's pedal to the metal from start to finish. I think that's just his personality: All out, all the time!

Even when it comes to business, Russell  can't sit still. He's worked in innovative ways to get his name out there. He collaborated with musician Daniel Ho on a pair of music CDs, for example. (They're great! It's music that actually matches the chef's cuisine.) To have that kind of entrepreneurial vision is really impressive. One of the neatest things about doing *Hawai'i's Kitchen*, in fact, is seeing first-hand the brilliance of our local chefs.

Russell is another local boy made good. His interest in cooking began as a child, when he helped his paternal China-born grandfather prepare Chinese dishes for family dinners. His grandmother on his mom's side, meanwhile, was born in Hawai'i, and she loved island-style favorites. Even as an award-winning chef, Russell still relies on her tips for preparing different local dishes. As for Russell's mom, her specialty was baking. In fact, Russell learned how to bake long before he started cooking.

He got his first cooking job at age 15, at a local drive-in. He then moved on to coffee shops, then restaurants, and then international clubs. This guy really paid his dues! His culinary career has taken him all around the globe, from Dallas to New Orleans, Canada to Hong Kong. Finally, he returned home and opened 3660 on the Rise in Kaimukī and Kaka'ako Kitchen, now located at Ward Centre.

With some chefs on our show, you have to walk them through everything. Russell, however, is one of those guys I call a "stand back" guest. I just stand back and watch, and every now and then I tell him when we have to break for a commercial!

Russell is a good talker, but he's a good listener, too. He's very savvy. When he sees that I want to comment on something, he'll pull back and let me have my say. I really like that in a guest, and the result is usually a very good show.

Snapper Carpaccio, Chinese-Style

8 oz.	snapper, sushi grade, thinly sliced
	salt, to taste
1 cup	dashi
1/8 cup	prepared teriyaki sauce
1-1/2 tbsp.	prepared ponzu sauce
1/4 cup	finely julienned ginger
6 tbsp.	extra virgin olive oil
1/4 cup	finely chopped green onion
4 tsp.	finely shredded nori
1 tsp.	toasted sesame seeds

Divide the snapper evenly among 4 plates, laying the slices in a circle. Season lightly with salt. Combine the dashi, teriyaki sauce and ponzu and ladle over the snapper, covering the plate. Top with ginger. Heat the olive oil in a saucepan until smoking. Drizzle the fish with the hot olive oil. The oil should sizzle. Garnish with green onions, nori and sesame seeds. Serves 4.

Pan-Seared Moi with Miso-Shiso Nage

3 tbsp.   vegetable oil
4   moi fillets, pin bones removed
            salt and pepper, to taste
2 tbsp.   toasted sesame seeds
2 tbsp.   black sesame seeds

Miso-Shiso Nage
1-1/2 cups fish stock
1/2 cup   white wine
1 tbsp.   coarsely chopped ginger
1 clove   garlic, halved
1 tbsp.   chopped shallots
3 tbsp.   white miso
2   shiso chopped leaves
1/4 cup   unsalted butter
            salt and pepper, to taste

To prepare the nage: Combine all the ingredients in a pot, except the butter, salt and pepper. Simmer over medium heat for about 10 minutes until reduced by half. Whisk in the butter; strain. Season with salt and pepper. To prepare the fish: Heat a frying pan and add oil. Score the moi and season with salt and pepper on both sides. Saute on medium high, skin-side down until the skin is crispy. Turn and saute until fish is cooked through. Place the black and white sesame seeds in a coffee grinder and grind to a powder. Remove the fish from the pan and dust with the sesame powder. To serve: Ladle 1/4 cup of nage onto each serving plate and place a moi fillet in the center. Garnish with corn relish or fried leeks and tempura shiso leaf. Serves 4.

Ginger-Crusted Opakapaka with Plum-Chili Sauce

4	opakapaka fillets, 6 oz. each
	kosher salt and black pepper, to taste
1/8 cup	grated ginger
1/8 cup	finely chopped green onion
1/8 cup	finely chopped cilantro
1-1/2 cups	panko
1/8 cup	vegetable oil or clarified butter

Plum-Chili Sauce

2 cups	plum wine
1 cup	rice vinegar
	juice of 1 lime
2 tbsp.	chopped scallion
2 tbsp.	chopped ginger
2 tbsp.	chopped shallots
3 tbsp.	Lingham chili sauce
3/4 cup	heavy cream
1-1/2 cups	unsalted butter, in pieces
	kosher salt and pepper, to taste

Season the fillets with salt and pepper. Combine the ginger, green onion, cilantro and panko. Press one side of each fillet onto the panko mixture, making sure that the crust is even across the fillet. Heat oil in a pan over medium heat. Fry the fillets, panko-side down, until golden brown. Turn and continue cooking until the fish is cooked through, about 5 minutes. To prepare the sauce: In a non-reactive saucepot, combine plum wine, rice vinegar, lime juice, scallion, ginger, shallots and Lingham chili. Simmer until reduced by half. Add the cream and reduce until thickened. Slowly whisk in butter. Strain and season with salt and pepper. To serve, ladle 1/4 cup of sauce into the center of each serving plate and top with a fillet. Garnish with a sprig of cilantro. Serves 4.

Grilled Duck Breast with Braised Daikon and Roasted Chicken Stock-Scented Dashi

| 4 | duck breasts, silver skin removed and skin scored |
| | salt and pepper, to taste |

Marinade
3 cups	water
1/4 cup	salt
1/8 cup	soy sauce
3	cloves garlic, halved
1-in. pc.	ginger, peeled and quartered
1/4 cup	brown sugar
1/4 cup	sliced shallots

Braised Daikon
4	daikon circles (3-inch diameter, 1/2-inch thick)
2 cups	Roasted Chicken Stock-Scented Dashi
1/8 cup	prepared teriyaki sauce

Roasted Chicken Stock-Scented Dashi
6 oz.	roasted or canned chicken stock
1-1/2 cups	dashi
1 oz.	unsalted butter
	salt and pepper, to taste

Combine marinade ingredients. Marinate duck for 6 hours. Bring a pot of water to a boil. Remove duck breasts from the marinade and place in plastic Ziploc bags. Seal the bags and place in boiling water. Turn off the heat and let the duck poach in the water for about 12 minutes. Remove and let rest 15 minutes. Season with salt and pepper. Grill on a charcoal or gas grill at medium heat, skin-side down to render the fat. Turn and grill until cooked through. Serves 4. To prepare dashi: Reduce chicken stock for about five minutes and add dashi. Simmer for another 4 minutes and whisk in butter. Season with salt and pepper. To prepare daikon: Simmer in dashi until cooked through. Keep warm.

3660 Chocolate Souffle Cake with Vanilla Ice Cream and Mocha Sauce

2 lbs.   bittersweet chocolate
1/2 lb.   sweet butter
16   egg yolks
1-1/2 cup sugar, divided use
12   egg whites
             vanilla ice cream

Preheat a convection oven to 325 degrees. Spray 20 6-ounce souffle cups with cooking oil and line the bottoms with parchment paper. Melt the chocolate and butter over a double boiler. Whip the yolks and 8 ounces of the sugar together until a ribbon forms. Do not overwhip. Fold chocolate into the yolk mixture. Whip egg whites with the remaining 4 ounces of sugar and fold into the chocolate mixture. Portion the batter into the souffle cups. Bake for 17 minutes. Remove and serve immediately with vanilla ice cream and Mocha Sauce.

Mocha Sauce
2 cups   heavy cream
1/2 cup   sugar
1 tbsp.   prepared chocolate syrup
2 tbsp.   instant coffee granules
1/2 tsp.   vanilla extract
6   egg yolks, beaten

Combine the cream, sugar, chocolate syrup, coffee and vanilla extract in a saucepan over medium heat. Right after the mixture comes to a boil, slowly stir half of it into the beaten eggs. Be sure to add the hot cream mixture gradually, to temper the eggs. Then pour the egg mixture into the remaining hot cream in the saucepan. Stir over medium heat for 30 to 45 seconds. Strain and cool. Extra sauce can be saved to serve with ice cream or other desserts.

'Ahi Tartare with Tobiko Caviar and Wasabi Oil

8 oz.	top-grade 'ahi, very finely diced
1/4 cup	extra virgin olive oil
1 tbsp.	finely diced green onions
1 tsp.	chopped capers
1/2 tsp.	grated ginger
	salt and pepper, to taste
4 tsp.	tobiko caviar, for garnish
8 stalks	chives, for garnish

Wasabi Oil
1 tsp.	wasabi
1/4 cup	olive oil

Combine all the ingredients except the garnishes. Season with salt and pepper. To prepare the Wasabi Oil: Combine olive oil and wasabi in a blender; blend until smooth.
To serve: Spoon tartare into 4 martini glasses. Drizzle with Wasabi Oil and garnish with caviar and chives. Serves 4.

Chinese Barbecue Duck Salad with Liliko'i Vinaigrette

1 cup	water
1/8 cup	white vinegar
1	duckling (4-1/2 to 5 lb.)
3 slices	ginger
1/4 bunch	green onions
1/4 bunch	cilantro leaves
2 tbsp.	soy sauce
1 qt.	hot water
1/4 tsp.	Chinese 5-spice
6 oz.	mesclun greens

Glaze

1/4 bunch	cilantro leaves
1/8 bunch	green onion, finely diced
2 cups	plum sauce
1 cup	soy sauce
1 cup	hoisin sauce
1 cup	honey
1/4 tbsp.	grated ginger

Put 1 cup of water and vinegar in a large pot and bring to a boil. Baste the duck with this mixture for 2 to 3 minutes, until the skin of the duck feels tight. Mash together the ginger, green onion and cilantro. Add soy sauce, hot water and Chinese 5-spice. Rub the duck inside and out very well with this mixture. Hang the duck in a cool area until the skin is dry, 7 to 8 hours. Preheat oven to 325 degrees. Roast duck 1 hour. Remove from oven and cool. To prepare the glaze: Mash the cilantro and green onion in a stainless steel bowl, using the back of a spoon. Add the remaining ingredients and mix well. Preheat oven to 350 degrees. Remove breasts from the duck. Brush breasts with glaze and bake about 15 minutes until golden brown. Slice. To serve: Toss mesclun greens with a drizzle of Liliko'i Vinaigrette. Garnish with the sliced duck. Serves 4.

Liliko'i Vinaigrette

	zest and juice of 1/2 lime
1 tbsp.	sugar
1/2 tsp.	freshly ground black pepper
1 clove	garlic
1	thin slice ginger
1 cup	rice wine vinegar
3/4 cup	passion fruit purée
3 cups	vegetable oil
2 oz.	honey

Combine all ingredients in a blender except oil and honey. Blend until smooth. Add oil slowly, then honey. Do not overmix.

Rock Shrimp and Watercress Tortellinis with Yuzu Butter Sauce and Sweet Soy Drizzle

1 cup	rock shrimp, coarsely chopped
1/2 cup	chopped watercress leaves
1 tbsp.	unsalted butter
1/4 cup	julienned onions
1/2 cup	white wine
2 tsp.	rice vinegar
1/2 cup	unsalted butter, in pieces
	salt and pepper, to taste
12	won ton pi wrappers

Yuzu Butter Sauce

1/4 cup	white wine
1/4 cup	rice vinegar
1 clove	garlic
1/2 tsp.	chopped shallots
1/2 tsp.	chopped ginger
1 tbsp.	chopped green onions
1/2 cup	heavy cream
1-1/2 tbsp.	yuzu (Japanese citrus juice)
1/2 cup	unsalted butter, cut into blocks
	salt and pepper, to taste

Combine rock shrimp and watercress in a bowl. Melt butter in a saucepot over medium heat. Add onions and saute until transparent. Add white wine and vinegar and reduce by half. Whisk in pieces of butter a little at a time. Season with salt and pepper and strain through a fine sieve. Add the onion mixture to the shrimp and watercress; mix until butter hardens slightly. Season with salt and pepper. Wrap in won ton pi, folding into triangles, then won ton shapes. Boil in water for about 3 minutes, or until won ton pi is cooked. Serves 4. To prepare Yuzu Butter Sauce: Combine wine, vinegar, garlic, shallots, ginger and green onions in a saucepot over medium heat. Reduce by half. Add cream and cook until thickened. Add yuzu and whisk until incorporated. Let simmer for about 2 minutes, then slowly whisk in pieces of butter. Season with salt and pepper. Strain and keep warm. Place tortellinis on plate, ladle Yuzu Butter Sauce over tortellinis and drizzle with Sweet Soy Chili Sauce.

Sweet Soy Chili Sauce

21 oz.	kecap manis (Indonesian soy sauce)
5 oz.	sherry
	zest and juice of 2 oranges
2 tbsp.	grated ginger
4	cloves garlic
4 oz.	Sweet Chili for Chicken

Combine all ingredients in a pot and simmer until thickened. Strain.

Chilled Tomato Bisque with Crabmeat, Tobiko Caviar and Avocado Timbale

4 tbsp.   extra virgin olive oil
1/2 cup   finely diced onions
3 cups   diced tomatoes, puréed
1-1/2 cups   chicken stock
1 tbsp.   chopped basil
             salt and pepper, to taste

Timbale
4 oz.   crabmeat
1 tbsp.   finely chopped chives
1 tsp.   lemon juice
1/2   avocado, diced
4 tbsp.   tobiko caviar
4   parsley leaves, for garnish

To prepare the bisque: Heat half the olive oil in a pot over medium heat. Add onions and saute until transparent with a tinge of brown. Add tomato purée, chicken stock and basil. Simmer for about 30 minutes over low heat. Purée the bisque in blender till smooth. Season with salt and pepper. Whisk in the remaining olive oil and chill. To prepare the timbale: Combine crabmeat and chives in a non-reactive bowl and toss. Add lemon juice and mix gently. Divide the mixture into 4 portions. Using a 1-1/2 inch round mold, place a layer of avocado, then crabmeat, pressing softly to level off. Top with caviar and garnish with a parsley leaf. Unmold each timbale in the middle of a soup bowl. Ladle chilled soup very carefully around the timbale. Serves 4.

Alan Wong

My admiration for Alan Wong goes beyond his accomplishments as one of Hawai'i's premier chefs. I also appreciate him because he's part of the Easter Seals *ohana*.

One of my sons, Shawn, has Down's Syndrome. In the first few years of Shawn's life, Easter Seals was always right there for us, helping us through the hard times. So I'll always be grateful to this fine organization, and I always try to do whatever I can to return the favor. To see Alan's involvement with Easter Seals just takes my respect for him to an even higher level.

As far as his culinary talents are concerned, what can I say? Alan enjoys an incredibly successful career as one of the true masters of Hawai'i Regional Cuisine. His ability to marry elements of different ethnic cooking styles with the finest Island-grown ingredients is unsurpassed.

Local culinary aficionados know that Alan got his start in Hawai'i in 1989, when he opened The Canoe House Restaurant at the Mauna Lani Bay Hotel & Bungalows on the Big Island. Just five years later, he was named one of 13 Rising Star Chefs in America for culinary excellence by Robert Mondavi Winery. And two years after that, Alan received the prestigious James Beard Award for Best Chef in the entire Pacific

Northwest/Hawai'i region. More recently, in 2002,
the Inaugural 2001 Wedgwood Awards honored
Alan as one of ten chefs nominated to represent
the U.S. in Paris for the title of World Master of
Culinary Arts.

Some resumé, eh?

But despite all his awards and accomplishments, Alan doesn't have a swelled head. He's all
about cooking, and he loves to teach. I mean, if
there were ever a professor in this bunch of
chefs we're featuring in this book, it would be
Alan. He really wants you to know what he
knows. Alan doesn't hold
back anything, while some
chefs of his caliber guard
their secrets like gold in Fort
Knox! He has a genuine
desire for you to understand
what he's doing. Some chefs
are very showy, and that's
great, but a lot of times you
would never be able to do their dishes at home.
But with Alan, no matter how beautiful his dish
is, he wants you to be able to actually cook it
yourself and sample it.

Alan has done several of our shows, and
we truly enjoy great rapport. I'm just delighted
whenever a guy of his stature drops by to do
Hawai'i's Kitchen.

Clear Tomato Gazpacho

1 tsp.	finely diced tomatoes
1 tsp.	finely diced cucumber
1 tsp.	finely diced red bell pepper
1 tsp.	finely diced green bell pepper
1 tsp.	finely diced celery
1 tsp.	finely diced fennel
1 tsp.	finely diced Maui onion
1 tsp.	finely diced water chestnut
1 tsp.	cooked shrimp
1 tsp.	cooked lobster
1 tsp.	cooked scallop
3/4 cup	Infused Tomato Water

Garnish

	julienned shiso
	julienned basil
	julienned green onions
3	Nicoise olives

Arrange each tsp. of the vegetables and seafood around a plate like a clock. Pour Infused Tomato Water in the middle of the plate and garnish. Serves 1.

Infused Tomato Water

5	tomatoes, coarsely chopped
1-1/2 tsp.	salt
1 tbsp.	Chili Pepper Water
2	cloves garlic, thinly sliced
6	fresh basil leaves
4 or 5	thin slices fennel bulb
	salt and pepper, to taste

In a blender, combine the tomatoes and salt and blend until smooth. Strain the liquid overnight: Place a disposable coffee filter or piece of cheesecloth into a strainer. Place the strainer over a bowl and pour the liquid through.Refrigerate and allow to strain slowly; do not press. The next day, reserve the tomato pulp for another use. Add the Chili Pepper Water, garlic, basil and fennel to the strained liquid. Season with salt and pepper. Refrigerate for at least 1 hour to allow the flavors to develop. Transfer to an airtight container; keep refrigerated. Makes 2-1/2 cups.

Chili Pepper Water

1/3 cup	cold water
1/2	clove garlic
2	red Hawaiian chili peppers or red serrano chili peppers, or 1 red jalapeno, halved and seeded
1 tbsp.	white vinegar
2 tsp.	minced ginger
pinch	salt
1-1/4 cups	water

In a blender, combine the 1/3 cup of water, garlic, chilies, vinegar, ginger and salt, then purée until smooth. In a saucepan, bring the 1-1/4 cups of water to a boil. Add the puréed mixture and return to a boil. Remove from the heat. When cool, transfer to an airtight container. Keep refrigerated. Makes 1-1/2 cups.

Wok-Charred Soy Beans with Garlic and Chilies

1 tsp.	minced ginger
1 tsp.	minced garlic
8 oz.	soy beans, cooked with the shell on
1	minced Hawaiian chili pepper
1 tbsp.	soy sauce
1 tsp.	oyster sauce
1-1/2 tsp.	sesame oil

In a hot wok, saute ginger and garlic until golden brown. Add soybeans and continue to cook until hot. Add chilies, soy sauce, oyster sauce and sesame oil. Stir fry for additional minute and serve immediately.

Shrimp and Clams with Chili-Lemongrass Black Bean Sauce

3	Manila clams, washed
3 pieces	shrimp (16/20 size), peeled and deveined
1 tbsp.	salad oil
1/2 tsp.	garlic, minced
1/2 tsp.	ginger, minced
2 tbsp.	onion, diced
2 tbsp.	lemongrass, sliced
1 tsp.	Chinese black beans, rinsed and drained
2 tbsp.	sherry
1 tbsp.	Thai chili sauce
4 tbsp.	snow peas
2 tbsp.	tomato, diced
8 tbsp.	penne pasta, cooked
2 tbsp.	chicken stock
3 tbsp.	butter
	salt and pepper, to taste

In a hot saute pan, sear clams and shrimp in salad oil. Add garlic, ginger, onion, lemongrass and Chinese black beans. Deglaze with sherry. Add Thai chili sauce, snow peas, tomato, pasta, chicken stock and butter. Cover pan and simmer until seafood is fully cooked and butter is melted. Season with salt and pepper. Add more Thai chili sauce if desired. Serves 1.

Pho Salad

2-1/2 oz.	roasted strip loin, chilled, thinly sliced, cooked medium rare
1	fresh jalapeno pepper, thinly sliced
1	shallot, peeled, thinly sliced
2	shrimp (16/20 size), cooked and cut into 1/4-inch dices
2 tbsp.	cooked somen noodles
2 tbsp.	chopped basil leaves
2 tbsp.	chopped cilantro leaves
1	basil sprig
	Hoisin-Sriracha Sauce

Arrange beef slices on an 8-inch plate as you would carpaccio. Zigzag the Hoisin Sriracha Sauce across the beef slices. Place the somen noodles in a neat pile on top of the beef and top with jalapeno peppers and shallots. Sprinkle the shrimp over the top. Garnish with cilantro and basil.

Hoisin-Sriracha Sauce
1/2 cup	hoisin
3/4 cup	sriracha

Combine sauces and pour into a squeeze bottle.

Truffle Poke Soy Mustard Beurre Blanc

6 oz.	big eye 'ahi
2 tbsp.	truffle oil, or to taste
1 oz.	minced truffle peelings
1 tbsp.	chives
	salt, to taste
	Sevruga caviar or other brand
1 slice	avocado, for garnish
	tapioca chip or any crispy chip, for garnish

Combine 'ahi, truffle oil, truffle peelings and chives, seasoning with salt to taste. Form into a cylindrical shape on a plate, using a ring. Carefully lift the ring. Spoon Soy Mustard Beurre Blanc around the plate. Top with caviar. Garnish with a slice of avocado and a tapioca chip.

Beurre Blanc

3/8 cup	minced shallots
6	white peppercorns
1-1/2 cups	white wine
1/2 cup	white wine vinegar
4	bay leaves
2 cups	heavy cream
3 lbs.	sweet butter, cold, cut into 16 pieces

Soy Mustard

4 tbsp.	dry mustard
2 tbsp.	warm water
5 tbsp.	soy sauce (preferably Yamasa)

Whisk the mustard into the water to make a smooth paste. Slowly stir in soy sauce until the mixture is smooth. Set aside. For the beurre blanc: In a heavy, non-reactive saucepan, add the shallots, peppercorns, white wine, vinegar and bay leaves. Cook over medium-high heat until au sec. Add cream and bring to a boil. Cook until mixture is thick and coats the back of a wooden spoon. Remove from heat. Whisk in butter, adding a piece after the previous piece is incorporated. Strain through a fine-mesh sieve. Slowly stir in the soy-mustard mixture to taste.

Korean-Influenced Curry with Coriander/Fennel Blend

2 tbsp.	salad oil
2	medium onions, sliced
4 tbsp.	Madras curry powder
12 cups	chicken stock
1 cup	Ko Choo Jang (Korean chili sauce)
2 cups	coconut milk
1-1/2 lbs.	kim chee
1/2 cup	Tamarind BBQ sauce
2	medium tomatoes, diced
2 cups	chopped cilantro leaves
2 cups	chopped basil
	kosher salt, to taste
2 tbsp.	coriander seeds
1 tbsp.	fennel seeds

For Coriander/Fennel Blend, heat seeds in a saute pan until fragrant, then grind in a spice mill or coffee grinder. Set aside. Heat salad oil in a pot until it is just about to start smoking. Add onions and saute until slightly browned. Add the Coriander/Fennel blend and curry powder. Saute until onions are cooked through and spices are fragrant. Add chicken stock and bring to a simmer. Add the Ko Choo Jang, coconut milk, kim chee, Tamarind BBQ Sauce and tomatoes and simmer for 1/2 hour. Add cilantro and basil; let simmer 30 more minutes.

Tamarind BBQ Sauce

1/2 cup	water
1/2 cup	sugar
1/4 cup	freshly squeezed lemon juice
1/4 cup plus 1 tbsp.	tamarind paste
2 tbsp.	honey
1 tbsp.	cayenne
1/2 tbsp.	ground cumin
1/2 tbsp.	ground coriander
1/2 tbsp.	fennel seed

Combine ingredients and mix well.

Linda Yamada

Leeward
Community
College
CULINARY PROGRAM

L inda Yamada is well respected by everyone in the restaurant business. She has cooked at several great eateries around the state, including the Beach House in Po'ipū on the island of Kaua'i. But the reason I thought it was important to include her in this book goes beyond her terrific culinary talents. A lot of chefs give back to the community, but Linda has taken that to a whole new level.

Basically, she's decided to step away from the restaurant business to teach the next genera-

tion of Hawai'i chefs. She's now an instructor at Leeward Community College's culinary program, helping up-and-coming young chefs learn all about the business. It's a great story — a culinary star returning to school to help the new generation — and I think it's important to recognize Linda for her efforts. I have no doubt that some of her students will someday be guests on *Hawai'i's Kitchen*. (And for that, I will be eternally grateful!)

I'll give you a little scoop: Just for kicks, Linda sometimes goes down to Colin Nishida's Side Street Inn and helps with the cooking. Just for kicks! That should tell you something about her passion for the business.

But then, that's Linda. She's a little firecracker. I mean, she's the type of person who likes to put her head down and get right to the job at hand. She's a worker.

I love having her as a guest on our show. We have sort of a running joke between us. I'm 6'4", you see, and she's 5'2" or 5'3". She'll be doing her thing on the set, going through her recipe step by step, and then I'll tell her, "Linda, will you please stand up?"

She's a great sport, though. She can take it, and she can dish it out too! That's the neat thing about Linda. She's a local girl to the max, but she's also got a style about her that's all her own.

Seared Sea Scallops and Green Papaya Salad with Cranberry Essence

12	large sea scallops
	sea salt and cracked black pepper, to taste
3 tbsp.	olive oil
5 to 6 oz.	salad greens
	fried corn tortilla strips (optional)
	Cranberry Essence

Green Papaya Salad

1 cup	finely julienned green papaya
1/4 cup	finely julienned carrot
1 tsp.	finely chopped garlic
2 tsp.	finely chopped fresh cilantro
2 tbsp.	fresh lime juice
1 tsp.	Thai fish sauce
pinch	sugar

To prepare the salad: Combine all the ingredients. Set aside. To prepare the scallops: Season the scallops with sea salt and pepper. Heat a saute pan until hot. Add the olive oil and sear the scallops on both sides until browned and the center is no longer translucent. Place salad greens in the center of each plate and top with a portion of papaya salad. Arrange 3 scallops around each plate and drizzle with Cranberry Essence. Fried corn tortillas strips may be used as garnish. Serves 4. Note: this is a gluten-free recipe.

Cranberry Essence
2 cups   red wine
2 cups   sugar
2 cups   cranberry juice

In a non-reactive pot, bring wine and 1 cup of the sugar to a boil. Simmer until the mixture achieves a thin syrup consistency (about 230 degrees on a candy thermometer). Meanwhile, in a separate non-reactive pot, bring the cranberry juice and remaining sugar to a boil and simmer to a thin syrup consistency. Combine the wine syrup and cranberry syrup. Cool to room temperature. If the syrup begins to harden, soften it by placing the syrup in a warm water bath.

Gazpacho with Shrimp Truffle Poke

2 cups	diced ripe tomatoes, seeds removed if desired
1 to 2 cups	tomato juice, depending on desired thickness of soup
2	cloves garlic
1 cup	diced, peeled and seeded cucumber
1/2 cup	diced celery
	salt and fresh ground pepper, to taste
2 tbsp.	extra virgin olive oil

Shrimp Truffle Poke

1/4 lb.	shrimp, deveined and poached, then coarsely chopped
1 tbsp.	minced white onion
1 tbsp.	minced green onion
1 tbsp.	minced cilantro
1/2 tsp.	coarsely chopped truffle peelings
	sea salt, to taste
1 tsp.	truffle oil

To prepare the gazpacho: Combine first five ingredients in a blender. Season with salt and pepper. Slowly whisk in olive oil to emulsify. Strain if desired. Chill for at least 6 hours.
To prepare the poke: Combine all the ingredients and chill well. To serve: Ladle gazpacho into chilled bowls and place a teaspoon of poke in the center. Serve immediately. Serves 4.

Herb-Roasted Pork Loin with Chipotle-Mango Sauce

1   boneless pork loin, cleaned
           olive oil
           Hawaiian salt and cracked black pepper, to taste
           fresh thyme sprigs
           fresh rosemary sprigs

Preheat oven to 375 degrees. Place pork loin on a roasting rack. Rub with olive oil and season with salt, pepper, thyme and rosemary. Roast for 20 to 30 minutes, or until medium rare. Remove from the oven and allow to cool. Slice and grill quickly on both sides. Serve with Chipotle-Mango Sauce.

Chipotle-Mango Sauce
1 pint   red wine
1 quart   mango purée
1/2 cup   brown sugar
1 gallon   veal stock
1/4 can   chipotle peppers in adobo sauce
            salt and pepper, to taste

Combine all ingredients in a pot. Simmer for 30 minutes, then blend.

Lemongrass and Kaffir Lime Leaf-Crusted Scallops with Citrus Butter, Chili Aioli and Braised Kaua'i Baby Bok Choy

12   scallops (10/20 count), dried on a paper towel
          vegetable oil

Crust
4 oz.   lemongrass (white/bottom of stem)
6   kaffir lime leaves
1 cup   fine panko

Citrus Butter
1/2 cup   dry white wine
1/2 cup   heavy cream
1 cup   butter
1 tbsp.   fresh lime juice
1 tbsp.   fresh lemon juice
           salt and pepper, to taste

Chili Aioli
1/2 cup   mayonnaise
1 tbsp.   sweet chili or sambal sauce
1 tbsp.   finely minced cilantro
1 tsp.   finely minced garlic
           salt and pepper, to taste

To prepare the crust: Preheat oven to 275 to 300 degrees. Place the lemongrass and lime leaves on a baking sheet. Dry completely in the oven. Process the dried lemongrass and lime leaves in a coffee or spice grinder until coarsely chopped.Combine lemongrass and lime leaf mixture with panko and set aside. To prepare the scallops: Heat a non-stick saute pan on medium-high heat. Coat the pan with a thin layer of oil. Bread each scallop with the crust mixture. Saute on both sides until the scallops are golden brown, then remove from the pan and set aside. To prepare the butter: Place the white wine in a saucepan over medium heat. Reduce by half. Add the cream and reduce by half again. Over low heat, add the butter slowly, stirring constantly and adding a new piece as each piece is incorporated. Do not let the sauce boil, as this will cause it to break or separate. Stir in the lime and lemon juices and season with salt and pepper. To prepare the aioli: Combine all the ingredients; chill. To serve: Spoon Citrus Butter onto the bottom of 4 serving plates. Arrange three scallops in a circle on each plate and top with Chili Aioli. The dish may be garnished with julienned green onion, black sesame seeds or kizami shoga or served with a rice or noodle dish. Serve immediately. Serves 4.

Seared Salmon and Braised Spinach with Roasted Garlic Sherry Sauce

6-8	garlic cloves
	olive oil
4	salmon fillets (3 oz. each)
	freshly ground pepper, to taste
1/2 oz.	sliced onions
1 oz.	sliced mushrooms
3 oz.	fresh spinach, cleaned
1/4 cup	sherry
4 to 6 tbsp.	whole butter, diced, at room temperature

Place garlic cloves in a saute pan with enough oil to cover. Simmer the cloves on low heat until soft. Remove the cloves and let the oil cool. Store in a jar. Heat a medium saute pan until hot. Add a few tablespoons of the garlic oil. Season the salmon with pepper. Sear quickly on both sides. Set aside. Saute the onions and mushrooms. Add the spinach. Deglaze the pan with sherry. Add the oil-roasted garlic cloves and butter. Can be served with rice, potatoes or pasta. Serves 2. Note: As a substitute for butter, 2 ounces of medium diced tomato may be used in the sauce instead.

Apple Banana Foster

1/2 cup	whole butter
1/4 cup	brown sugar
1/4 tsp.	ground cinnamon (optional)
4	apple bananas, peeled and halved lengthwise
4 slices	banana or mango bread
4 scoops	vanilla ice cream

Heat a saute pan over medium heat. Add the butter and allow to melt without browning. Add the sugar and cinnamon. Allow to reduce to the consistency of syrup. Add the banana halves and cook for 3 minutes. Arrange 2 banana halves around each slice of bread. Scoop ice cream on top of the bread and drizzle syrup over the ice cream. Serve immediately. Serves 4.

Index

About the Host

One of Hawai'i's best-known personalities, Brickwood Galuteria wears many hats. Besides his role with *Hawai'i's Kitchen*, he is a popular radio host, Hōkū Award-winning recording artist, actor (he appeared in the critically acclaimed 1998 film, *Beyond Paradise*), spokesman, community servant — and now author. A graduate of The Kamehameha Schools, Brickwood resides in Honolulu.

SHARE
THE HAWAI'I'S
KITCHEN COOKBOOK
WITH FAMILY
AND FRIENDS!

Watermark Publishing
1088 Bishop Street, Suite 310
Honolulu, Hawaii 96813

Toll-free 1-866-900-BOOK
sales@bookshawaii.net

Please send to:

Name _____ Phone _____

Address _____

City _____ State _____ Zip _____

$10.00 per copy x _____ $ _____

Shipping & handling* $ _____

TOTAL ORDER $ _____

❏ Check enclosed, payable to Watermark Publishing

❏ Charge my credit card   ❏ VISA   ❏ MC   ❏ Amex

                        ❏ Discover   ❏ Diner's   ❏ Carte Blanche

Card no. _____ Exp. date _____

Signature Required _____

* $4 for one copy, $2 for each additional copy